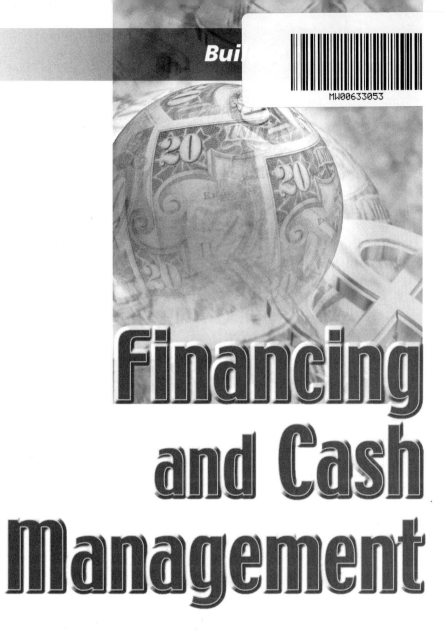

Buil

Financing and Cash Management

Dennis J. Rourke

A Service of

NAHB

BuilderBooks™
National Association of Home Builders
1201 15th Street, NW
Washington, DC 20005-2800
www.builderbooks.com

Financing and Cash Management
Dennis J. Rourke

ISBN 0-86718-546-5

© 2003 by BuilderBooks™
of the National Association of Home Builders
of the United States of America

Cover design by Armen Kojoyian
Printed in the United States of America

Cataloging-in-Publication Data available from the Library of Congress

Disclaimer
This publication is designed to provide accurate and authoritative information in regard to the subject matter covered. It is sold with the understanding that the publisher is not engaged in rendering legal, accounting, or other professional service. If legal advice or other expert assistance is required, the services of a competent professional person should be sought.
—From a Declaration of Principles jointly adopted by a Committee of the American Bar Association and a Committee of Publishers and Associations.

For further information, please contact:
BuilderBooks™
National Association of Home Builders
1201 15th Street, NW
Washington, DC 20005-2800
(800) 223-2665
Check us out online at: www.builderbooks.com

12/02 SLR Production/ Data Reproductions Corp., 1500

About the Author

Dennis Rourke built his first house at the age of twenty-two. During his career, he has held senior management positions with both small- and large-volume home building companies and he has owned and operated his own medium-volume home building and land development company for almost 25 years. His experience has centered on residential land development, home building, and the major renovations of existing homes. In addition to developing ground, he has built custom homes, custom speculative homes, and production housing of all types across all price ranges. As a home builder, he has earned the reputation of one who is and has been dedicated to quality construction, pro-active customer care, and the well being of his employees. Mr. Rourke considers management practice to be the most critical requirement for success as a home builder.

Mr. Rourke is a graduate of the American University in Washington, D.C. He holds a Bachelor of Science degree in Business Administration with a double major in real estate and business management. He is author of *The American Home Builder and the Housing Industry* and *Construction Management for the Residential Project Manager*.

BOOK PRODUCTION

Financing and Cash Management was produced under the general direction of Gerald Howard, NAHB Executive Vice President and CEO, in association with NAHB staff members Michael Shibley, Executive Vice President, Builder, Associate, and Affiliate Services; Greg French, Staff Vice President, Publications and Non-dues Revenues; Eric Johnson, Publisher, BuilderBooks; Theresa Minch, Executive Editor; and Jessica Poppe, Assistant Editor.

*This book is dedicated to the failed opportunities,
lost dreams, anxiety, frustration, financial losses, and embarrassment experienced by those who
have endured the hardship of bankruptcy as either a debtor or a creditor.*

CONTENTS

Preface   xi

Part I: Planning   1
1 The Importance of Planning   3
2 Strategic Planning   15
3 Financial Planning   23

Part II: Financing   37
4 Sources of Capital and Methods of Financing   39
5 Construction Financing and The Loan Proposal   55

Part III: Cash Management   71
6 Managing Cash and Reducing Risks   73
7 Financial Controls and Insolvency   99

Appendices
A A Long-Term Plan for Growth and Development   121
B A Sample Financing Proposal   143
C NAHB Chart of Accounts   147

Glossary   159

References   169

Index   173

PREFACE

Facing insolvency and the potential for bankruptcy is the most difficult position that management can encounter. In well-managed companies, the conditions that could produce such devastating circumstances are generally identified early and resolved before they can produce such a critical or fatal condition. Unfortunately, in many small- and medium-volume home building companies, the conditions that produce insolvency are not always recognized and the strategic action that is required to protect the company from the inability to pay its debts and discharge its financial obligations is not always understood.

In such cases, management often exacerbates the condition by extending payment terms, increasing debt, and otherwise concealing the problem in an effort to buy time and hope for extraordinary relief. Creditors and others that have routinely done business with the company lose respect for management, employees become ineffective and concerned about their own futures, quality plummets, and the ability to meet financial obligations to owners, lenders, investors, employees, contractors, subcontractors, and suppliers becomes apparent. The results can be devastating both financially and emotionally.

It is my hope that this book will help provide the knowledge and direction that home builders and their financial officers require in order to avoid insolvency or bankruptcy. Learning the discipline that combines quality planning with precise execution is a prerequisite for success in any business enterprise. The key resources of any organization are people and money, but performance depends largely on how those resources are employed. By combining a management structure with the ability to plan, organize, direct, and control effectively, with the knowledge of how money is raised, invested, spent, tracked, controlled, and measured, home builders can usually avoid that potentially fatal condition that we call insolvency.

To the uninitiated, the challenge of home building is to complete a single house and recover profit; to those seasoned home builders who understand the dynamics of a building company, the challenge is to knit together an effective business plan that will provide the stability and growth required by any on-going business enterprise. Continuity, stability, profitability, investor satisfaction, and the ability to meet financial commitments are of primary concern.

Financial plans are based on reason, logic, and strategic thinking. They are the basis for effective management and without them, management lacks direction and the ability to use benchmarks to evaluate performance.

PART I

1 THE IMPORTANCE OF PLANNING   3

2 STRATEGIC PLANNING   15

3 FINANCIAL PLANNING   23

CHAPTER 1

THE IMPORTANCE OF PLANNING

Planning is the foundation of success. It helps provide purpose, direction, and financial stability for any organization and it permits individuals operating within that organization to maintain control of personal growth and development. Most business plans are based on innovation and focus largely on the conversion of that innovation to opportunity, profits, and security. They create discipline, harness the effort and energies of staff, provide benchmarks, and, over the long-term, provide the basis for ongoing operations.

Most home builders recognize the importance of preparing detailed working drawings, specifications, and scopes of work before they start a construction project, but too often, builders fail to develop the formal business plans, policy, and management practices necessary to limit errors, reduce risks, and properly direct the effort of their companies. Just as working drawings, specifications, and scopes of work establish a road map that ensures a successful construction project, a well-conceived business plan will help ensure the successful administration and management of a business.

The art of successful management practice demonstrated by a well-conceived business plan is considerably more difficult to acquire than most disciplines in business, and it has a greater impact on the survival of a new business or an existing business experiencing intensive growth. Four out of five, or 80 percent, of new ventures fail, but a well-conceived plan can reduce those odds considerably.

THE PURPOSE OF PLANNING

The purpose of planning is to organize thoughts, ideas, strategies, and resources based on facts, to achieve both personal and business goals and objectives. An effective business plan that includes both well-conceived strategic and financial planning will provide the best template for success. Too often, we fail to provide the critical information that will enable employees to actively participate in the growth and development of our businesses. By crafting an effective business plan that reflects the input of each staff member, we can achieve clarity of purpose that is unique to well-managed companies. If you want your employees to support your effort, you must tell them where you are going and how you will get there. You must also permit them to participate in the creation of the plan.

THE ENTREPRENEUR AND INNOVATION

Well-conceived strategic and financial plans are a requirement for the healthy growth and development of homebuilding companies. The first step in developing a turnaround management program for a home building company in trouble is to create a well-conceived business plan. These plans become the template for success in well-managed companies.

Entrepreneurial spirit and innovation are the lifeblood of all free economies and the businesses within those economies. The desire to compete and the willingness to focus on solutions that create efficiency, provide value, and position a company in the market are keys to its long-term success. Often, these driving forces are provided by a select few in the well-managed company, but they are the foundation of its business plan. Although each employee should be given the opportunity to contribute, entrepreneurial spirit and innovation typically seem to come form the "big picture people" rather than those who tend to be more structured and controlled in their thinking. That is not to say that group dynamics is not important in the planning process. On the contrary, it is the best way to formulate and develop professional business plans. However, if professional business managers want to be successful contributors in the areas that formulate direction and provide the required innovation, they must maintain a sense of urgency, accept business risks as though they were their own, participate in the financial success of the business, look for opportunities, and remain focused on the direction of the enterprise as well as the day-to-day activity.

THE ENTREPRENEUR

An entrepreneur is one who plans, organizes, operates, and assumes the risk of a business venture with the expectation of realizing profit; one who shifts resources from areas of low productivity and yield to areas of higher productivity and yield. The need for overachievement drives most entrepreneurs, and home builders are entrepreneurs of the first order. They must inspire controlled innovation and the entrepreneurial spirit in their organizations. Good practices include focusing on opportunity, generating an entrepreneurial spirit in the management team, and developing planning seminars or meetings during which senior staff and both employees and strategic partners can contribute. Through such efforts, the entrepreneur can leverage the knowledge and experience of his staff and those with whom he does business.

PRINCIPLES OF INNOVATION

Innovation is the creation of something new and different; it is the specific instrument of entrepreneurship and it is often reflected in business plans. Innovation is both conceptual and perceptual, which means that it usually results from looking, asking, and listening. Most innovators tend to be opportunity-focused and not risk-focused, which can produce dire consequences to the home builder who does not measure risks carefully and allow others to participate in the development of the business plan. For innovation to be effective, it must be simple and well focused; purposeful, systematic innovation begins with an analysis of opportunities.

Sources of innovative opportunity can often result from a number of conditions including the following:

◆ New knowledge resulting from both scientific and nonscientific sources

◆ Unexpected changes in an industry or a marketing structure

◆ Unexpected success or failure

◆ Demographic changes

◆ A significant event

◆ A process need

◆ The incongruity between reality and what it is assumed or ought to be

◆ Changes in perception, mood, or meaning

Change and innovation should be a natural result of growth and development in the well-managed company. Financial success often depends on innovation in highly competitive markets. The mark of a mature building company is one that takes advantage of innovative opportunity and is quick to move from mistakes, failures, and misdirected effort. These are also the companies that tend to maintain a policy of abandoning, that which is outworn, obsolete, or no longer productive; in short, they are forward thinking.

THE PURPOSE OF THE BUSINESS PLAN

A business plan offers the opportunity to refine strategies and make mistakes on paper; it provides a basis for measuring performance, and it is required to raise money. Some of the *benefits* of a well-conceived business plan include the following:

◆ Helps management set priorities and direction; it provides a track for the business to run

◆ Applies the strengths, skills, abilities, and interests of the management team

◆ Saves time and minimizes effort

◆ Helps reduce waste and unnecessary expenses

◆ Reduces stress and unnecessary risks

◆ Increases the probability of profits

◆ Attracts and influences others such as owners, investors, lenders, senior employees, trade contractors, and suppliers.

In addition to ensuring the profitability of the company, a well-conceived plan will also help the company avoid uncontrolled growth that causes bankruptcy—a condition known as "growing into bankruptcy." Nothing will do more to protect the assets of a company than the creation of a well-conceived business plan.

After having said that business plans must reflect entrepreneurial spirit and innovative thinking, it should also reflect an acceptable level of conservative thinking. The plan will be reviewed by a number of people with different perceptions and purposes, and each will reach their own conclusions regarding risks. Each participant in the creation of a business plan must be guided by conservative thinking that is supported by facts. This point was made by Peter F. Drucker, who has become the father of modern management, in a single, simple statement: "There are old pilots, and there are bold pilots. But there are no old, bold pilots."

In summary, a well-conceived business plan will provide:

◆ Basis for raising capital

◆ Evaluation of and avoidance of risk

◆ Improved business performance through the direction of effort

◆ More effective decision-making

◆ Basis for variance reporting

◆ Structure and planning of new activities and ventures

SOURCES OF INFORMATION

A company will obtain the facts necessary to support conclusions established in a business plan from both internal and external sources. Using professionals such as accountants, attorneys, and marketing and management consultants to help improve a business plan is important, but such professionals should never create such a plan for a builder. Such plans should be created by the builder and his or her staff, and they should reflect the maturity and thinking of the organizations that prepare them. This fact should be critical to anyone reviewing the plan with the intention of measuring the potential for success.

Internal Sources

Internal sources may include information contributed by existing staff or others, such as strategic partners, who support your efforts. Excellent sources of information include:

◆ Trade contractors

◆ Suppliers

◆ Lenders

◆ Developers

◆ Settlement attorneys

External Sources

External sources of information also should be incorporated in a business plan. External sources of information typically include:

◆ Trade organizations such as local Home Builder Association (HBA) or National Association of Home Builders (NAHB)

◆ The Small Business Administration

◆ Local libraries

◆ U.S. Department of Commerce

◆ Local realtors

◆ Consultants

◆ Outside research organizations

THE FORMAT

Business plans for home builders must deal with both long- and short-term considerations, and they must be delivered in a professional presentation. They are a reflection of the maturity of the company and its perception of itself. Others who will review your plan have their agendas within which you must fit. Look for a confluence of agendas and understand your agenda, as well as the agenda of others who participate in the activities of your business. Business plans create a statement regarding the culture of the company, and they create clarity for the management team; once the management team understands the goals of the company and how it intends to accomplish those goals, it will be able to communicate this information to others.

Long-term planning for home builders may cover a period of five years, and *short-term planning* may cover a period of two years. Long-term planning establishes goals that are major, significant, and specific, and those goals should drive activity, which will achieve success through disciplined implementation. Setting the right long-term priorities and then implementing them will demonstrate a level of strategic effectiveness. An example of such a long-term goal might be to produce 25 percent of production or 200 units in active adult products within five years. *Short-term planning,* on the other hand, will be more detailed with more specific information related to projects and projections. Nothing will do more to improve group dynamics than working and agreeing on a list of shared values that are reflected in the detail of short-term plans.

Such plans not only galvanize the team, but also allow then they to think about creative ways to enhance the plan channel the congruent energy that will develop successive revisions of the plan. Both long- and short-term planning is an ongoing requirement. Performance against the plan must be reported to senior managers on a regular basis, and formal business plans should be reviewed, analyzed, adjusted and reissued every year. The planning function is ongoing and should maintain the focus of the management team throughout the year. It should be discussed in staff meetings, and evaluation of innovative opportunities should be the responsibility of each senior staff member. This process enables companies to measure performance at all levels.

THE PRESENTATION

The presentation of the business plan must be professional and provide not only the summaries and financial statements that represent conclusions, but they must also provide the facts and schedules from which such summaries were derived. Such plans should include the following.

COVER SHEET AND TABLE OF CONTENTS (SEE APPENDIX A)

The cover should make a statement that is relevant to the company and its vision. It should demonstrate a high level of sophistication and professionalism.

OVERVIEW OR EXECUTIVE SUMMARY

The purpose of this section is to present the big picture followed by supporting detail. It should summarize the goals and objectives and establish financial targets of performance. Each part of the plan must be linked with the overview or executive summary, and in total, the plan should include a substantial amount of fact, available data, and studies to support the conclusions presented in the overview or executive summary.

The overview or executive summary should include a statement of purpose. Such a statement should define what the company is and where it wants to go, and it should include a market-driven mission statement that establishes the vision of the company's future based on both internal and external components.

THE ORGANIZATION

This section should include a general business description that outlines the legal structure of the company (or its various entities), its culture, its products and services, profit centers, new products under development, its customer and warranty service program, lot inventories, and its attitude towards speculative construction.

THE MARKETING PLAN

The marketing plan should present both general and specific information related to the market and that information should then be carefully woven into a strategy and tactics (consisting of process and procedures) designed to maximize market share. General information should include:

♦ Definition of the market and the opportunity target

♦ Survey of the competition including absorption rates and unit profiles (square footage, features, sales prices, quality, and general specifications)

♦ Supporting information, such as demographics and industry studies including median household income and the number of households

♦ Other market research information; this is often provided by consultants

♦ Letters of recommendation (particularly as they relate to custom homes and remodeling work) and positive survey results, brochures, reviews, or articles related to the products and services of the company

Specific information contained in this section should also include those items that bring focus to the general information including the following:

♦ Market strategy statement

♦ Site analysis for each proposed or current project

♦ Evaluation of the market potential for each project in terms of market size, the level of competition, possible market share, and anticipated gross revenue per unit

♦ Product design and pricing that includes only those features that the market is willing to pay for and not those that a staff member may think are important

♦ Sales forecasts including total projected sales, an evaluation of market share, and a customer profile

♦ Feature marketing activities such as advertising, model home programs, and brochure development

♦ Sales promotion program

♦ Defined public relations program for the company

OPERATIONS

This section should include a discussion of current operations as it relates to feasibility studies, the production process, product development, post-settlement service, and company policy in general. These are all critical areas of operation and will help answer questions related to the quality of management and the company's ability to achieve its plan. When it is complete, this section should demonstrate that management understands the benefits of careful production planning and that they work in a market-driven industry; a higher level of efficiency results from careful production planning, and business plans in general are driven by the market and the company's ability to capture market share.

MANAGEMENT AND THE MANAGEMENT STRUCTURE

This section should discuss total management in terms or theory, principles, and practices, as well as identifying the management structure. It should include: 1) an organization chart, 2) a brief biography of each founding entrepreneur, active investor, key employee, and key advisor. In large companies, it should also include a brief biography of each director and member of the advisory board, and 3) a five-year salary schedule.

The strategic and financial plans of a company should reflect ethical behavior and a strong sense of responsibility to others. In that regard, this section should include an acknowledgement of the ethical responsibilities of employees. Individual values are projected in business plans and those plans must reflect a desire for excellence, a willingness to provide service, and respect for the individual. Business ethics can be thought of as a company's attitude and conduct toward its employees, customers, community, vendors, creditors, investors, and stockholders; they are standards of conduct or moral behavior and some simple statements of acknowledgement will provide a comfort level for some who will read the business plan.

In addition to providing information regarding the management structure and statements insuring ethical behavior, this section should describe basic management practices. These practices convert management theory and principles into action in the organization. Some current management practices for home builders include the following:

◆ Using a horizontal or lateral organizational network with a soft vertical alignment; focus on those with strong leadership skills, empower them, and encourage participation in management

◆ Compensating key management personnel with some or all of the following:

   ◆ competitive base salary

   ◆ benefits such as health insurance, paid holidays, personal days, and vacations with pay

   ◆ incentive bonuses based on performance

   ◆ personal development program that may include seminars, academic course work, and/or participation in NAHB International Builders' Show

   ◆ perks such as an auto or truck allowance, cellular phones

   ◆ 401k profit sharing program (which may not be selective and must be made available for all company employees); performance-based incentives will improve quality, financial controls, customer satisfaction, also help cultivate a team spirit

◆ Maintaining a lean overhead to allow flexibility; using outsourcing for some specific requirements in the areas of accounting, legal, sales, marketing, computer support, and consulting services. Consider leased equipment as opposed to making large fixed investments in heavy equipment, automobiles, or office equipment

◆ Maintaining a positive perspective and handling both negative and positive situations in a helpful, supportive way

◆ Forming a cooperative with other smaller home builders with the following benefits:

   ◆ Larger size improves consumer confidence, market awareness, and stability

   ◆ Volume purchasing reduces costs and often improves the quality of subcontractors and suppliers

   ◆ Sharing marketing expenses improves sales costs

   ◆ Sharing architectural plans reduces the costs related to plan inventories

CAPITALIZATION

This section should, again, discuss the legal form and manner of financial participation for the company and its various entities. Most home builders develop complicated structures to limit liability, maintain more positive control, and limit taxes. In most cases, larger home builders maintain separate entities for each major project to provide separate accounting, restrict the access to information related to overall operations, to prevent the co-mingling of funds, and to limit liability. These conditions must be disclosed in any business plan that includes the entire company in scope.

The capitalization of a homebuilding company is critical to its growth and development. Responsible companies will maintain a reasonable balance between debt and equity capital. An acceptable debt ratio (total liabilities divided by total assets) should fall between 63 and 69 percent.

In cases in which the business plan is intended to raise capital for specific projects, some statement of capital requirement is necessary. These capital requirements must be clearly stated, and the plan must demonstrate both the need and the method of repayment.

FINANCIAL PROJECTIONS

The purpose of the financial section of the business plan is to formulate a credible, comprehensive set of projections reflecting the anticipated financial performance of the company. Documents presented in this section typically include a life of project forecast, an income and expense statement, and a cash budget (cash flow projection). If such projections are carefully prepared and convincingly supported, they become one of the most critical yardsticks by which the company's business activities will be measured.

ATTACHMENTS

Typical attachments that might be incorporated in a business plan include a short history of the company, a policy manual, miscellaneous marketing material, and a confidentiality agreement.

THE IMPORTANCE OF THE FINISHED PLAN

The finished business plan for an organization includes a considerable amount of confidential information. While it is intended to provide critical information for those who have a need, it could be potentially damaging in the hands of a competitor, and it should not be available for most companies, individuals, or employees. A copy of the complete plan should be reserved for investors, owners, lenders, senior employees, and others who might have such a critical need. In all cases, a confidentiality agreement must be executed and retained by the company to ensure that the information contained in the plan will remain confidential.

Finished business plans may be presented in total or in various parts as the need dictates. The company should provide whatever information is necessary, but maintain a sense of security regarding the total plan. Not all of the information will be required or requested by those who will ask to see it.

CHAPTER SUMMARY

Planning is the foundation of success. It helps provide purpose, direction, and financial stability for any organization and permits individuals operating within that organization to maintain control of personal growth and development. Most business plans are based on innovation and focus largely on the conversion of that innovation to opportunity, profits, and security. They create discipline, harness the effort and energies of staff, provide benchmarks, and over the long-term, provide the basis for ongoing operations.

A well-conceived business plan will include both long-term (5 years) and short-term (2 years) planning and it will be delivered in a very professional presentation. It is a reflection of the maturity of the company and its perception of itself.

The presentation of the business plan must be professional and provide not only the summaries and financial statements that represent conclusions, but they must also provide the facts and schedules from which such summaries were derived. A typical business plan should include a cover sheet and table of contents as well as the following sections:

An Overview or Executive Summary: The purpose of this section is to present the big picture followed by supporting detail. It should summarize the goals and objectives and establish financial targets of performance. Each part of the plan must be linked with the overview or executive summary and in total, it should include a substantial amount of fact, available data, and studies to support the conclusions presented in the overview or executive summary

The Organization: This section should include a general business description that outlines the legal structure of the company (or its various entities), its products and services, profit centers, new products under development, its customer and warranty service program, lot inventories, and its attitude towards speculative construction.

The Marketing Plan: The marketing plan should present both general and specific information related to the market and that information should then be carefully woven into a strategy and process designed to maximize market share.

Operations: This section should include a discussion of current operations as it relates to feasibility studies, the production process, product development, post-settlement service, and company policy.

Management and the Management Structure: This section should discuss total management in terms or theory, principles, and practices, as well as identifying the management structure. It should include: 1) an organization chart, 2) a brief biography of each founding entrepreneur, active investor, key employee, and key advisor. In large companies, it should also include a brief biography of each director and member of the advisory board, and 3) a five-year salary schedule.

Capitalization: This section should, again, discuss the legal form and manner of financial participation for the company and its various entities in cases in which the business plan is intended to be used to raise capital for specific projects, some statement of capital requirements are required. These capital requirements must be clearly stated and the plan must demonstrate both the need and the method of repayment.

Financial Projections: The purpose of the financial section of the business plan is to formulate a credible, comprehensive set of projections that reflect the anticipated financial performance of the company. Documents presented in this section typically include a pro-forma income and expense statement, a pro-forma balance sheet, individual project budgets, and cash flow projections.

Attachments: Typical attachments that might be incorporated in a business plan include a short history of the company, resumes of key management personnel, a policy manual, and a confidentiality agreement.

The finished business plan for an organization includes a considerable amount of confidential information. Although it is intended to provide critical information for those who have a need, it could be potentially damaging in the hands of a competitor, and it should not be available for most companies, individuals, or employees. A copy of the complete plan should be reserved for investors, owners, lenders, senior employees, and others who might have such a critical need. In all cases, a confidentiality agreement must be executed by the recipient and retained by the company to ensure that the information contained in the plan will remain confidential.

CHAPTER 2

STRATEGIC PLANNING

Strategic planning is translating innovative leadership with vision into an agenda by linking the firm's vision, strategy, tactics, and implementation plans to gain a competitive advantage. It is focused planning coupled with disciplined action. Management must assume nothing, prepare for the unexpected, and stay ahead of the trends that are recognized by creating such action plans. This is accomplished by applying of policy, procedures, and processes that are developed as tactics.

STRATEGIC PLANNING

Vision sets direction and allows us to create the strategies that develop tactics. Most businesses are driven by one or more employee with vision, who then uses management personnel to lead the company to new levels of organizational effectiveness. Leadership begins with innovation, strategic planning, communication, the use of technology, and above all else, the ability to orchestrate events and resources to accomplish specific goals that result from the vision.

Strategic thinking enables us to position our businesses and take advantage of market conditions, management expertise, opportunities, and other circumstances affecting the growth and development of our companies. One of the primary characteristics of a well-managed company is the ability of its managers to think in the future; that is, to anticipate events and conditions based on current activity, the probability of future events, and the results of current actions. Without this ability, a manager is not capable of strategic thinking or adequate financial planning.

Well-managed companies must create strategies and plans for adapting and innovating in a changing business environment; strategies and plans that are *driven by the consumer,* who provides the opportunity for our success. Like most businesses, change is a constant requirement for success in homebuilding, and it must be facilitated through structured, multi-step methodologies that require systematic and comprehensive planning. Strategic plans should identify the required changes and provide for the orderly implementation of such change.

In his latest book, *The Essential Drucker,* Peter F. Drucker has the following to say about innovation as a practice.

Strategic planning is an essential process or carefully orchestrated scheme designed to achieve specific goals through the proper application of resources.

Vision is the creative capacity or foresight to perceive the potential for an event or outcome based on current facts and conditions.

"... *contrary to popular belief in the romance of invention and innovation, 'flashes of genius' are uncommonly rare. What is worse, I know of not one such 'flash of genius' that turned into an innovation. They all remained brilliant ideas.*"

"*The purposeful innovation resulting from analysis, system, and hard work is all that can be discussed and presented as the practice of innovation. But this is all that need be presented since it surely covers at least 90 percent of all effective innovations.*"

With regard to entrepreneurial strategies, he says:

"*There are four specifically entrepreneurial strategies.*
1. *'Being fustest with the mostest'*
2. *'Hitting them where they ain't'*
3. *Finding and occupying a specialized 'ecological niche'*
4. *Changing the economic characteristics of a product, a market, or an industry*
These four strategies are not mutually exclusive."

THE STRATEGIC PLANNING PROCESS

There are four fundamental steps required to develop effective strategic plans:

◆ **Vision Formulation.** Identifying and articulating a strategic business vision that will serve the company over a five-year period.

◆ **Strategy Development.** Formulating a business strategy that will achieve the vision over a two- to three-year period.

The professional knows how to create both strategic and financial plans, as well as how to execute those plans and monitor the results. Establishing goals offers distinct benefits: 1) they drive the enterprise, 2) they point staff and management toward the best and smartest strategies and tactics, and 3) they permit management by objective. Reducing cycle-time, improving referral sales, and improving net margin are all significant goals for home builders.

◆ **Tactical Planning.** Determining the best way to implement the vision and strategic plan over the next one to two years; tactics are reflected in the policy, procedures, and processes (all of which help to create a culture) established by the company.

◆ **Implementation.** Implementing the strategy and tactical plans over a one-year period by operating on a daily basis in accordance with those plans.

All who participate in the planning, as well as those who will evaluate such plans, must recognize that strategic planning is an extremely potent resource for an enterprise, and it has a great deal to do with its preservation, growth, and maximization of effort. Along with a timetable for achieving objectives, a strategic plan must also identify all of the critical risks or obstacles that may prevent its achievement. By examining the needs of the company and then identifying potential problems as well as opportunities, the company can then select the most effective alternatives.

DETERMINING THE NEEDS

Begin the planning process by identifying the needs of the company. Understand who benefits from your business and where they can be found. Stakeholders include a broad group of individuals, companies, or interest groups that are affected, influenced, or controlled by the operation of the business. This group includes:

◆ Purchasers

◆ Homeowners

◆ Employees

◆ Stockholders

◆ Investors

◆ Lenders

◆ Sales brokers and agents

◆ Settlement attorneys

◆ Architects

◆ Engineers

◆ Contractors

◆ Subcontractors

◆ Suppliers

◆ Communities in which we build

Experienced planners will consider the stakeholders carefully because these individuals and companies are not only affected, influenced, and controlled by the plan, but they also represent potential resources that can provide support for the plan.

Planners should also understand the benefits and services that are critical to the success of their businesses and how these benefits and services should be provided. A good example of the creative thinking that may be stimulated by such considerations, might be an effort to seek investment capital from one or more of your trade contractors, or perhaps, to create a title company with your current title attorney to provide a higher quality of service while establishing a secondary source of revenue. Creative thinking may also lead a builder to understand the need to provide proactive customer care, which is quickly becoming a top priority for most home builders; now is the time to identify the need and provide for a delivery system.

*The **strategy** might be to develop a trade partnership program to improve quality and cycle time. The **tactics** might include one-on-one meetings with the principles of these businesses, trade partnership luncheons, performance awards, and a current pay policy with checks distributed twice a month (on the 10th and 25th).*

A strategic plan should include adequate consideration for the product, the operation, and the growth and development of each employee who will participate in the plan. Homebuilding companies are complicated structures and require significant focus during the strategic planning process. Some examples of specific strategies to address include the following.

Land Acquisition and Development Strategies

A critical aspect in the growth and development of any homebuilding company, these strategies will include everything required to ensure an adequate supply of finished lots.

Market Strategies

These are strategies that largely result from observing, listening, and interpreting information; they often originate from facts developed from market studies (that should include a competitive analysis), surveys, and focus groups. Market strategies are designed to increase sales and create perceived value for homebuyers. Among other things, they define the market target and the buyer profile, set market share targets and absorption rates, and provide the means for industry recognition.

*The **strategy** might be to improve quality and prevent extraordinary repairs and callbacks after settlement. The **tactics** might include establishing a formal quality assurance program with a written checklist executed by the construction manager before concealment and requiring more thorough frame and floor checks, as well as a pre-drywall walkthrough with the purchaser.*

Product Development Strategies

It is management's responsibility to continue searching for a *substantial and sustainable competitive advantage,* and this effort is often reflected in its product strategies and then included in its product mix, designs, specifications, scopes of work, and option strategies, as well as in the process used to create them. Applying architectural, engineering, and management skills to design and refine products and services that meet the planning requirements is critical to the success of home builders. Well-managed home builders will establish a design team that includes both sales and production employees to manage new product development. They will also validate designs and encourage the participation of other staff members and, perhaps, focus groups to ensure the success of the product.

Pricing Strategies

An effective pricing strategy will typically include a provision for option incentives, the establishment of pricing for options and extras, and a well-conceived strategy for price increases based on an anticipated market response; effective pricing should first be established based by an evaluation of the competition and a determination of *what the market will bear,* but pricing should never be established without careful consideration for costs and the resulting net margin.

Developing price based on preliminary, pre-construction, and final budgets will ensure accuracy with respect to costs.

- ◆ **Preliminary pricing** *during the feasibility study before financing*
- ◆ **Pre-construction pricing** *after bids have been obtained, just prior to the start of construction*
- ◆ **Final pricing** *based on the substantial completion of a speculative home or model*

Cost Reduction Strategies

These usually include interdependent strategies designed to ensure accurate estimating, competitive vendor pricing, accurate billing, the elimination of duplicate payments, the reduction of waste, and an auditing procedure to protect against theft.

Human Resource Strategies

These strategies will typically include those required to recruit, develop, manage, and train a departmentalized team, which will have a significant impact on the success of the company. The material contained in an employee orientation manual typically outlines the tactics resulting from these strategies.

E-Business Strategies

These are strategies that largely relate to collaboration and information management that may focus on the development of an integrated, web-based information management system, based on current technologies that will improve revenue opportunities and decrease operational inefficiencies. Often topics here will include website development, e-mail technologies, high-speed internet access, a security protocol, the creation or improvement of a cellular phone network, and improvements to the back office and accounting business systems. It is important to note here that the Internet offers a unique solution for home builders who have a critical need for collaboration and information sharing.

According to Peter F. Drucker, who has spent his life defining management, "The effective executive does not make many decisions. He solves generic problems through policy." The formulation of policy is a strategic activity that produces a collection of statements, which amount to tactics, designed to support the goals of any business enterprise.

Management Strategies

These include strategies that are related to planning, organizing, directing, and controlling the activities of the company that will reduce risks, improve productivity, and create efficiency. They typically include the formulation of policy, a safety plan, and an employee training manual, as well as procedures for sales and settlement processing, production administration, reporting, and post-settlement service, to mention a few.

Customer Care and Public Relations Strategies

These strategies should include those that are established to ensure customer satisfaction, provide referral sales, and increase the standing of the company in the community.

THE IMPORTANCE OF STRATEGIC THINKING

Integrate all of the important elements needed to produce a working plan: 1) formulate the vision, 2) develop the strategies after evaluating strengths, weaknesses, opportunities, and potential threats, 3) set objectives and plan the tactics, and 4) implement the plan strategies. Many builders will use surveys and focus groups to help develop strategies and measure results.

Strategic thinking should become part of the daily routine of every professional manager. The ability to take action today that will produce an advantage down the road is an extraordinary skill, and it can be achieved through a simple exercise designed to promote strategic thinking. Ask management staff to devote one half hour a day over the next week to develop strategies and then share them at a regularly scheduled staff meeting. Repeat this exercise from time-to-time or make it a standard topic on such meeting agendas and enjoy the response.

Some other typical strategies that may develop as a result of this exercise may include:

◆ Promote custom home building and remodeling to extend income potential beyond the limits of current credit capacity; by developing these profit centers, a builder can use the credit of his purchasers when he has borrowed to his capacity.

◆ Maintain precise systems and document effort to resolve complaints with your most difficult customers, those who represent a substantial potential for disputes. Assign responsibility for such purchasers to senior managers who possess the most knowledge and experience and document efforts to over-service and provide more attention than a reasonable person might expect.

◆ Maintain a current pay status as a matter of policy to avoid a critical cash position resulting from short-term cash flow disruptions. This will improve the support of trade partners and give the company some potential relief within reasonable credit terms in the event of a real cash flow pinch.

◆ Avoid a copycat product and include features that may be offered by others as options, and then develop a pricing strategy that will create something distinctive in the market and secure a competitive advantage. You may forfeit some potential additional margin on options to create perceived value in the mind of the consumer.

◆ Avoid risks related to land that is not well located—under power lines or adjacent to major highways; although there are many considerations in a feasibility analysis, location is still number one.

◆ Low-volume home builders may Consider building a house every four or five years to increase net worth through "sweat equity" if you are a low-volume home builder.

Housing markets are fluid and can change quickly. Home builders must remain aware of the ongoing need for strategic planning and those plans must be review and improved on an annual basis. By creating the framework for strategic plans in a small group of senior employees and then expanding it to include others who should be given the opportunity to provide input on an ongoing basis, the home builder can not only take advantage of the potential for the contribution of others, he or she can also validate established policy and facilitate its acceptance.

CHAPTER SUMMARY

Strategic planning is the result of translating innovative leadership with vision into an agenda by linking the firm's vision, strategy, tactics, and implementation plans to gain a competitive advantage. It is focused planning coupled with disciplined action.

Management must assume nothing, prepare for the unexpected, and stay ahead of the trends that are recognized by creating strategic plans.

Establishing goals offers distinct benefits: 1) they drive the enterprise, 2) they point toward the best and smartest strategies and tactics, and 3) they permit management by objectives.

Popular thinking has identified four fundamental steps in the strategic planning process:

1. **Vision Formulation**—identifying and articulating a strategic business vision that will serve the company over a five-year period
2. **Strategy Development**—formulating a business strategy that will achieve the vision over a two-to three-year period
3. **Tactical Planning**—determining the best way in which to implement the vision and strategic plan over the next one to two years; tactics are reflected in the policy, procedures, and processes (all of which create a culture) established by the company
4. **Implementation and Operations**—implementing the strategy and tactical plans over a one-year period by operating on a daily basis in accordance with those plans (policies, procedures, and processes)

Understand who benefits from your business and where they can be found. Stakeholders include a broad group of individuals, companies, or interest groups that are affected, influenced, or controlled by the operation of the business. This group includes purchasers, homeowners, employees, stockholders, investors, lenders, sales brokers and agents, settlement attorneys, architects, engineers, contractors, subcontractors, suppliers, and the communities in which we build.

A strategic business plan should include adequate consideration for the product, the operation, and the growth and development of each employee who will participate in the plan. Unless the goals of a strategic plan provide adequate rewards for its participants and the market that it serves, it is inadequate.

Some examples of specific strategies that should be addressed, include the following: 1) land acquisition and development strategies, 2) market strategies, 3) product development strategies, 4) pricing strategies, 5) cost reduction strategies, 6) human resource strategies, 7) e-business strategies, 8) management strategies, 9) customer care and public relations strategies, and 10) financial strategies.

Strategic thinking should become a daily routine for every professional manager. The ability to take action today that will produce an advantage down the road is an extraordinary skill.

Housing markets are fluid and can change quickly. Home builders must remain aware of the ongoing need for strategic planning and those plans must be review and improved on an annual basis. By creating the framework for strategic plans in a small group of senior employees and then expanding it to include others who should be given the opportunity to provide input on an ongoing basis, the home builder can not only take advantage of the potential for the contribution of others, he or she can also validate established policy and facilitate its acceptance.

CHAPTER 3

FINANCIAL PLANNING

The financial plan organizes financial objectives, and it confirms the potential for financial success based on assumptions and conditions that have been documented in the strategic plan. A financial plan that reflects the strategic thinking of an organization is a fundamental requirement for an effective business plan and becomes the central focus of the business plan.

Financial plans are created based on a formal process that primarily includes the participation of the owners or directors and the senior staff. Financial plans that were originally developed for feasibility purposes continue to be modified, revised, and adjusted to reflect new strategies. This is an ongoing process that requires the focus of management. Comprehensive strategic and financial plans are a prerequisite for both financing and the ultimate success of the company.

THE PURPOSE OF FINANCIAL PLANNING

Accounting is the financial language of business and well-conceived financial plans are the key to creating comfort in the minds of owners, investors, lenders, key employees, and others. Financial plans demonstrate financial conclusions based on facts. Financial planning provides the roadmap or template for future business operations. Such planning is ongoing, and it is reflected in formal financial plan summaries, worksheets, and schedules, which are prepared and revised periodically for measuring performance. Financial planning establishes financial goals for the company and provides milestones for the evaluation of progress against those goals. Such planning begins with the development of strategies that will improve the stability of the company and ensure a higher level of performance and success. Once the strategies have been set and tactics have been identified, it is time to create the forecasts, worksheets, schedules, and summaries that will reduce these strategies to a standardized plan of action. Careful and deliberate financial planning will ensure the success of the company.

STRATEGIC FINANCIAL PLANNING

Forecasting and planning is a primary activity of the financial manager or accounting department. In the case of most small-volume home builders, this function falls on the shoulders of an owner or president of the company. Financial strategies should be formulated very carefully and deliberately. They should be considered, discussed with other staff members and consultants, and then included in the financial plans for implementation.

THE PRIMARY OBJECTIVE

The primary objective of any financial manager is to *maximize the return on invested capital,* while minimizing risks. Financial strategies and initiatives that *increase revenue or market share* and *reduce costs* to produce a higher level of profitability include the following strategies:

INCREASED REVENUE STRATEGIES

Land strategies might include creating a strategic partnership with one or more land developers, establishing the ability to develop ground, using purchase money trusts to increase the ability to afford new ground, hiring a land acquisition specialist, or perhaps creating joint ventures with land owners.

Market strategies might include expanding into new markets, developing a custom homes and/or renovation profit center, increasing the effectiveness of an existing marketing program, using consultants to increase the knowledge base, opening a selection center that will better organize the process and generally improve the level of option income, or perhaps, establishing a pre-sale program on new projects that will enable early sales (and production).

Product strategies might include using focus groups to help define the product, developing new designs that are more responsive to the market, using more than one architect to establish variety, carefully defining the product before meeting with an architect, involving both sales and production staff in the design process, or perhaps, using the internet for new product collaboration.

Cost Reduction Strategies

Productivity may be improved by changing the culture, including performance incentives in compensation packages, replacing marginal employees, modifying the work environment, creating detailed job descriptions, creating a training program for employees, or using written agendas for all staff meetings.

Operating efficiency may be improved by more clearly defining policies and procedures, improving back office systems, better defining processes, improving communications, developing a partnership program with trade contractors and suppliers, improving the bidding and contracting process through the use of written specifications and scopes of work, increasing production quality through the use of checklists and homeowner involvement, creating a streamlined process for special option requests, developing a strategic partnership with a title company that establishes a participation in title fees, or reducing the cost of funds through credit line financing and additional investment.

Waste reduction strategies may include tighter control of lumber, tighter management of casual labor, improving the product through value engineering, tighter control over the importation or exportation of dirt, a more deliberate system of solid waste disposal, or moving toward a paperless work environment.

EXAMINING THE CAPITAL STRUCTURE

Many strategic considerations are related to the capital structure of a company. The legal structure of the company may limit some considerations and make other considerations more critical. A sole proprietorship or limited liability company will not have the same capital structure as a corporation; and a *"C" corporation* may not have the same structure as an *"S" corporation*. Typically, large public companies are "C" corporations, and small closely held companies are more likely to be "S" corporations, sole proprietorships, or limited liability companies. Each will have a different cost of capital and different opportunities to raise capital. To further complicate matters, many builders use a mix of ownership entities to limit personal liability. The mix of both equity and debt capital must be evaluated and clearly understood.

Corporations typically raise equity capital through the sale of stock and then issue bonds and obtain ADC loans and/or credit lines to finance operations. Sole proprietorships and limited liability companies, on the other hand, are typically funded with equity provided by the owners and then rely on a mix of investment capital and debt capital obtained from the same ADC and/or construction lines of credit lenders. Both short- and long-term strategies that protect ownership interests and reduce the cost of funds are critical to the growth and development of homebuilding companies. Financial planners must also understand both the current and proposed conditions that affect the cost of capital. The local economy, the availability of investment capital, and current standard borrowing rates are very important considerations.

Corporations must consider the balance of equity funds resulting from the issue of common and preferred stock as opposed to the debt resulting from bonds, credit lines, and ADC loans. They must examine the impact of debt on the value of the company, and they must consider the dilution of ownership created by capital strategies. This is particularly true when it comes to convertible debt, convertible preferred stock, or debt with detachable warrants; these tools are typically used as enticements for an investor to offset some risk related to operations, but they all dilute current stockholder's equity. The tax positions of corporations may also have some influence on debt decisions and should be considered carefully.

Regardless of the legal form of the homebuilding company, builders must recognize the importance of maintaining adequate cash reserves and understand

In a recent study of small-volume home builders, (delivering less than 25 homes) conducted by Mark Hutchings, a breakdown of business organizations revealed the following types:

SCorporations	*40.78%*
Sole Proprietorships	*27.65*
CCorporations	*18.72*
LLCs	*9.50*
Partnerships	*3.07*

Of this group, only 12.26% had a written business plan.

According to a recent survey conducted by the National Association of Home Builders, the Debt to Equity Ratio (total debt ÷ owner's equity) for the industry was 3.42. It was 3.54 for builders building less than 26 units, 3.36 for builders who delivered more than 25 units, and 4.39 for custom home builders. When measured by income performance, it was 2.80 for the top 25% of home builders and 5.11 for the bottom 25%.

that the ability to create revenue or earnings before taxes is often based on the ability of a company to borrow at below market rates or to otherwise maintain a very low cost of funds. This has a significant impact on competition in the housing industry, when you consider that the major public homebuilding companies maintain an extremely low cost of money compared with smaller or closely held companies; they maintain significant pools of retained earnings and many have been able to obtain debt capital at extraordinarily low costs based on their financial performance

With regard to investment capital, it is important to understand that attitudes toward risk are relevant and significant and that the time-value of money is critical. The outcome of any proposal is uncertain, and the cost of funds will often depend on the perceived risks. Well-conceived business plans will reduce such risks in the mind of the investor and instill a confidence that should result in a lower cost of invested capital. Financial planners must also take advantage of the time-value of money; funds at different times have different values and such values will be of critical interest in the mind of an investor.

THE PRESENTATION OF FACTS

With regard to the facts presented in financial plans, it is important to remember the following:

◆ The facts presented in the financial plans must be consistent with the entire business plan.

◆ Projections must remain within industry averages and ratios, and not reflect exceptional performance.

◆ Although performance may be exceptional as a matter of history, plans should remain conservative to present a realistic picture to potential lenders or investors.

◆ *Assumptions are critical* to any financial plan and should be carefully highlighted and supported by facts, independent studies, professional advice, or detailed planning.

◆ Inadequate profit margins are one of the leading causes of financial distress.

◆ Gross margin, pre-tax profit, and return on investment are all critical numbers for those who review financial plans.

It also is critical to remember that financial plans should include a financial disclaimer. It may be a simple statement that places the reviewer on notice that the material has not been audited and is intended for the internal use of the company. In most cases the following statement will be sufficient:

"The information presented in this financial plan has been developed for management purposes only. It has not been audited and the Company therefore makes no representations regarding its accuracy."

THE CHART OF ACCOUNTS

A chart of accounts is a detailed list of the various kinds of assets, liabilities, revenues, expenses, and equity that a business might encounter. It provides structure for the accounting system—a complete format for the organization of the financial information that is required to make important decisions. The chart of accounts recommended by the National Association of Home Builders has become the industry standard (Appendix C). The adoption of this chart of accounts is strategic because it enables the company to better analyze its performance against industry standards and to use benchmarking as a management tool.

THE FINANCIAL PLANNING PROCESS

The financial planning process for companies includes both financial planning for the feasibility analysis of new projects and the review and revision of continuing projects that survived the initial feasibility analysis. Current project plans are reviewed and modified and integrated with proposed future revenue and expense strategies to create the company's new business plan.

THE FEASIBILITY ANALYSIS

A feasibility analysis for a new project will include: detailed analysis of the site, the market, the local jurisdiction, and the terms of purchase. Market studies, soils studies, environmental impact studies, and site characteristics (and restrictions) are examined in formal written reports and then incorporated in a final presentation. From these reports, strategies are formulated, and a financial analysis is prepared. Product and pricing strategies are established based on a careful evaluation of the market, the competition, and both current and future economic conditions. Such product and pricing strategies will then be reduced to absorption rates and sales projections, which will drive the financial plan. By establishing an *absorption rate* with monthly *sales forecasts,* a projection of production *starts* can then be anticipated and *cycle-time* (the anticipated construction time in process) can be evaluated. This will allow the projection of *closings* or settlements, which completes the timeline for the project.

Once sales, starts, and closings have been established, budgets can then be created for land, development costs, both direct and indirect construction costs, financing expenses, marketing *hard* and *soft costs,* and general

The analysis of facts that is necessary to accurately forecast sales, starts, and closings must not be underestimated. Significant and detailed research is necessary to minimize the potential for failure. An experienced reviewer of financial plans for home builders will examine these specific forecasts carefully to determine the level of consistency and whether the forecasts are supported by facts.

administrative costs. This provides the basis for a pro-forma income and expense summary as well as a cash budget or cash flow analysis summarizing proposed monthly activity.

Income and expense summaries should include percentages of gross revenue and ratio summaries of critical elements. Costs are typically projected based on historical data, unit cost estimates, and established pricing. While budgets are superficially a prediction of the results for any given planning period, they are also the financial expression of the company's detailed plans for that period. They must be created in the proper strategic context and should be prepared precisely within the framework of the objectives, strategies, and plans of the company. The presentation should reflect the benefits and consequences of the company's activities and actions. Budgets and forecasts must be based on explicit assumptions that cover important uncontrollable factors that are used to develop the numbers, and they must then be reviewed frequently and adjusted where necessary to reflect ongoing change.

THE COMPANY FINANCIAL PLAN

Business plans typically include financial plans that reflect the financial performance of various projects (and/or entities), which represent the entire scope of operations for an organization. Such plans are prepared to provide a complete financial analysis of the activities of the company to isolate strengths and weaknesses and to inform those who must defend the value of the plan to investors. The plan should demonstrate the company's ability to reduce risks, which is the most valuable skill that an organization can have when it comes to raising capital or planning for survival. It should be prepared to demonstrate the potential return on invested capital and the potential risk to principal, which is the overriding concern for all investors. The strength of any financial plan depends on a conservative expectation of performance. Numerical entries must be based on direct data, trends, and models. Goals must be achievable based on available resources.

During the preparation and presentation of the financial plan, it is important to maintain a focus on the purpose of the plan. An experienced investor will carefully consider the risks in terms of:

◆ Management expertise

◆ Track record

◆ Both background and reputation of senior personnel

◆ Current business activities

◆ History of dispute resolution

◆ Outstanding litigation

◆ Current ownership

◆ Degree and quality of strategic and financial planning

Financial plans for public companies to determine the market value of stock will focus on book value, earnings per share, and probable price/earnings ratio. It is important to keep the interests of stockholders and investors in mind. The plan should be prepared in a coherent, efficient, and timely process.

PLANNING DOCUMENTS

Many planning documents are typically incorporated into the financial plan for a homebuilding organization. These are usually summary documents that are supported by budgets, worksheets, and schedules that would only be made available upon request. Some fundamental summary documents include the following.

LIFE OF PROJECT PROJECTIONS

Most home builders will prepare month-to-month projections that will cover the life of the project. These forecasts typically cover a 24 to 36 month timeframe and include the life of the project. They are summaries created during the feasibility period that are then reviewed and revised throughout the life of the project. They include the unit sales, starts, and closings projected on a monthly basis, as well as the anticipated income and expenses.

In most cases, these projections are established under the direction of a chief financial officer, a director of accounting and finance, or a controller and are formally approved by the owners or directors. They are typically prepared in concert with the various department heads and/or responsible staff members. To be effective, they should include the input of individual staff members and department heads responsible for sales and marketing, production, purchasing, customer service, and finance. When these individual projections are rolled up and integrated into a master plan for all of the company's operations, they become the cash budget for the company.

PRO-FORMA INCOME STATEMENT

The *pro-forma income statement* is a traditional and simple summary of projected income.

Financial plans should include a consolidated, common size income statement that shows the costs, expenses, and profit as a percentage of sales for every related entity.

CASH BUDGET

A cash budget containing the cash flow projections for a company is the best planning tool to reduce risks, establish financial goals or benchmarks, and organize the effort to continue of the business enterprise. This is particularly true for the small-volume and custom home builders. The cash flow process is an erratic, circular system of asset transformation. Cash is used to purchase goods and services that are used in manufacturing and marketing products that are then sold, and upon closing or settlement are returned to cash. Conventional lenders and other creditors need to be satisfied that the projected

INCOME AND EXPENSE COMPARISON

All	Builders	Av. Small-Volume Builders <26*	Av. Builders >25	Production Av Top 25% of Builders**
Sales Revenue	100.00%	100.00%	100.00%	100.00%
Less Cost of Sales	80.13	82.16	79.50	77.23
Land & Development Costs	NA	14.58	18.21	NA
Direct Const Costs	NA	62.70	57.85	NA
Indirect Const Costs	NA	2.54	3.00	NA
Other Revenue Costs	NA	2.33	0.43	NA
Gross Profit Margin	**19.87%**	**17.84%**	**20.50%**	**22.77%**
Less Expenses				
Financing Expense	2.19	2.12	2.34	1.99
Sales & Marketing Expense	5.70	3.09	6.22	5.67
Gen & Administrative Exp	3.88	3.28	3.87	3.58
Net Revenue*	**8.11%**	**9.35%**	**8.07%**	**11.54%**

*Includes only those small-volume builders with land costs.
**The top 25% of all builders that participated in the program in terms of profitability.
***Net Revenue before taxes including owner's compensation
Note:This table was prepared from information contained in the *2001 Cost of Doing Business Study* published by the Business Management Department of the National Association of Home Builders. It is an accepted format that summarizes the conclusions of a number of worksheets, schedules, and projections for an individual project or an organization as a whole. It is an organized and accepted presentation of the anticipated results of activity that has not yet occurred and it is the primary focus of any financial plan review.

cash flow will be adequate to cover debt service throughout the term of a project or obligation and still provide an adequate margin for contingency conditions.

Cash flow forecasting is a critical activity that requires deliberate consideration and extreme care. If the conditions reflected in the forecast are not conservative, accurate, or complete, the value of this discipline is destroyed and the resulting decisions could be inaccurate. It is critical to check the numbers (including the electronic formulas used in spreadsheets), challenge the conditions, consider the assumptions, and review the input carefully to ensure the accuracy of this decision-making tool.

With the flexibility provided by simple computer spreadsheet software, "what if" scenarios can be easily applied and evaluated before finalizing the plan or approving a property for purchase. Often, such scenarios will highlight alternative terms or conditions of a deal that will improve its probability of success. As a result of the ease of recalculation, such evaluations will not only stimulate the modification of such terms and conditions before final feasibility approval, but they may also help provide a stronger course of action for the company, which can be reflected in the business plan.

A good cash budget format will reflect:

◆ Income from all sources, including the sale of houses, start-up capital provided by the company and/or its investors, loan disbursements, and income from miscellaneous sources

◆ Anticipated disbursements for all categories, including loan repayments, investor distributions, curtailments on land trusts, construction costs, and operating costs

◆ Resulting profits

THE NEED FOR ACCURACY

Everyone who participates in the creation of financial plans must understand that the financial plans will be reviewed and dissected by experts. These experts will rely on the information that has been provided, but in most cases, they will analyze the information carefully with the intention of validating its accuracy and unearthing the assumptions, which may be weak or invalid. Errors in calculations or the presentation of the material will convey a lack of understanding and focus, which should produce serious concern on the part of the reviewer. Using assumptions that are unrealistic and not supported by facts should also present concern, but the concern will most probably be for the level of risk presented by the plan. In either case, a unique opportunity will probably be lost—the opportunity to demonstrate a higher level of management practice and to achieve the objectives for which the plan was created.

REALISTIC AND ACHIEVABLE PLANS

Plans must be conservative and establish realistic goals for the company.. If planners are too aggressive, they set themselves up for failure. If they are too conservative, they are not taking advantage of opportunities and may encourage a lower level of productivity. The business plan *must be realistic and achievable* and resist the temptation to be too aggressive. By involving others in the creation of the plan, you establish a consensus. Those senior managers who participate in the planning process must understand clearly that the performance level established by the plan is exactly what they will be held accountable for. Most business plans are monitored on a monthly basis and actual results are measured against the plan.

Usually, it is my experience that those who prefer aggressive plans tend to fall short, but they do usually maintain a higher level of productivity and may even accomplish more than most. However, if the plan is aggressive, this strategy must be stated early in the plan documents, and it will become critical for both owners and managers to protect the staff from unreasonable stress; aggressive plans tend to create more enthusiasm among staff, but they can also produce unreasonable demands. In such cases, formal quarterly reviews and adjustments are critical, and it will also become more important to keep others informed of the progress against the plan. Aggressive plans can also produce disappointment among stockholders and a challenge when it comes to tax planning.

BREAK-EVEN ANALYSIS

Although a break-even analysis is probably seldom, if ever, used by larger production builders, it can be a very effective tool for the small- or medium-volume and custom home builder. Such an analysis will help builders understand the impact of fixed costs commitments on their operations. To compute the break-even point, costs must first be classified as fixed or variable, and the contribution margin must be established. *Fixed costs* are those that remain constant regardless of volume, and *variable costs* are those that are attributable directly to the sale, such as direct construction costs. The *contribution margin* is the percentage of each sales dollar that is left after variable costs are deducted:

$$\text{Contribution Margin} = \frac{\text{Sales} \times \text{Variable Costs}}{\text{Sales}}$$

Once the fixed costs, variable costs, and contribution margin have been determined, the break-even point can be calculated by dividing the total fixed costs by the contribution margin:

$$\text{Break-Even Point} = \frac{\text{Total Fixed Costs}}{\text{Contribution Margin}}$$

Example, If a company projects sales revenue of $12,000,000 with a fixed cost of $1,200,000, and a profit margin of 10%, the break-even point would be $6,000,000. With an average sale of $400,000, the company would have to deliver 15 units to break even. For example:

.20	=	$\dfrac{\$12,000,000-\$9,600,000}{\$12,000,000}$
$6,000,000	=	$\dfrac{\$1,200,000}{.20}$
15	=	$\dfrac{\$6,000,000}{\$400,000}$

Ratio Analysis

A ratio is an expression of a mathematical relationship between one quantity and another. Ratios only gain significance when they are compared with:

◆ Previous ratios of the same company

◆ Some predetermined standard

◆ Ratios for a benchmark company in the same industry

◆ Standard performance ratios for the industry within which the company operates

Ratio analysis is becoming more important as industry standards begin to emerge for companies of similar volume, profit centers, and general composition. Most home builders attach little value to ratio analysis unless they are one of the large public companies or intend to go public. In fact, all building companies should make some attempt to maintain comparisons of ratios from year-to-year. Maintaining ratios is a good discipline and will help keep management focused on meaningful goals and financial stability.

The most significant source for industry standard ratios and financial information is the National Association of Home Builders. The Association will periodically conduct a home builder survey and publish the results in a publication known as the *Cost of Doing Business Study*. In addition to this study, some other sources of ratios may include:

◆ Financial service organizations, such as Moody's or Standard & Pours, which provide financial statistics, histories, and current developments for publicly reporting companies

◆ Credit collecting organizations, such as Dun and Bradstreet, which publish key business ratios for most industries

◆ Investment and brokerage companies, which often provide comparative statistics relating to individual companies, selected companies in an industry, or an entire industry

◆ Trade publications, such as *Builder* magazine

◆ Benchmark companies from other market areas with which you may exchange operating information

Although ratios are usually difficult to find for direct comparison, home builders should evaluate ratios during the planning process and prepare a formal ratio analysis of each operating year to help understand shifts in their businesses. Such measurements can help identify problems and provide management with standards, which may become important to others trying to evaluate the business. Some key ratios include the following.

Home builders are usually classified as

◆ *small volume, building fewer than 26 units,*

◆ *production, building more than 26, or*

◆ *custom, building one-of-a-kind homes. NAHB sponsors a program known as the NAHB 20 Clubs, that is designed to bring together 20 builders from non-competing markets twice a year to exchange information and ideas that will improve their management practices.*

Liquidity
Current Ratio = Current Assets ÷ Current Liabilities
Anywhere between 1 and 2 is acceptable. According to a recent study, the industry average for all home builders was 1.36.
Working Capital Turnover = Total Revenue ÷ Working Capital
Industry experts believe that this should be less than 30 with a target of 8 to 12 times.

Profitability
Gross Profit Margin = Gross Profit ÷ Total Revenue
Industry experts believe that a target of 19 to 21 percent is acceptable. According to a recent study, the industry average for the top 25 percent of home builders (those with the highest net profit margins) was 22.77 percent; the median for this same group was 19.50 percent.
Net Profit Margin = Net Income ÷ Total Revenue
Industry experts generally believe that a target of 8 to 10 percent is acceptable.

According to a recent study, the industry average for the top 25 percent of home builders (those with the highest net profit margins) was 10.47 percent; the median for this same group was 9.39 percent.

Return Ratios

Return on Assets (ROA) = Net Income ÷ Total Assets

Most will try to achieve at least 30 percent. According to a recent study, the national average for all home builders was 11.77 percent.

Return on Equity (ROE) = Net Income ÷ Owner's Equity

Most will try to achieve at least 50 percent. According to a recent study, the national average for all home builders was 52.08 percent.

Indebtedness

Debt to Equity = Total Debt ÷ Owner's Equity

Anywhere between 2 to 4 is acceptable. According to a recent study, the industry average for all home builders was 3.42.

Debt Ratio = Total Liabilities ÷ Total Assets

Industry experts recommend a target 63 to 69 percent.

Leverage Ratios

Assets to Debt = Total Debt ÷ Total Assets

Industry experts recommend a target between 62 and 68 percent.

Assets to Equity = Owner's Equity ÷ Total Assets

Industry experts recommend a target between 32 and 38 percent.

Asset Efficiency

Current Assets to Total Assets = Current Assets ÷ Total Assets

Industry experts recommend a target between 64 and 69 percent.

Net Fixed Assets to Net Worth = Net Fixed Assets ÷ Owner's Equity

Industry experts recommend a target between 42 to 50 percent.

Financial planners should understand the importance of these ratios to those who will review the final business plan, as well at those who will evaluate the actual performance of the company. Indebtedness ratios and the liquidity ratios are of particular importance to lenders because they measure a company's solvency or its ability to meet its cash obligations. Lenders are very interested in the indebtedness and leverage ratios because they measure how heavily the assets are financed by lenders as opposed to the owner's resources; the higher the leverage, the higher the risk to the lender. The financial analyst will look for deviations in computed ratios and then look for the causes. In addition to ratio deviations, a financial analyst might also conduct a specific purpose examination, which may include a cash flow, gross margin, break-even, or return on investment analysis. Proper financial analysis employs the use of tools and techniques to examine past and current financial positions in order to evaluate the potential and future risks associated with a particular company. Such evaluations produce information about trends and relationships, the quality of earnings, and the strengths and weaknesses of a particular company's financial position.

CHAPTER SUMMARY

In addition to being required by investors and lenders, the financial planning contained in the overall business plan for an organization serves as a reality check for management, it organizes financial objectives, and it confirms the potential for financial success based on assumptions and conditions that have been documented in the strategic plan.

The ability to create a financial plan that reflects the strategies set forth in the strategic plan of an organization is the basis for an effective business plan. In well-managed homebuilding companies, financial plans are created based on a formal process that includes the participation of the owners and the senior staff.

Financial planning establishes financial goals for the company and provides milestones for the evaluation of progress against those goals. Such planning begins with the development of strategies that will improve the stability of the company and ensure a higher level of performance and success. Once the strategies have been set and tactics have been identified, it is time to create the forecasts, worksheets, schedules, and summaries that will reduce these strategies to a standardized plan of action.

The adoption of an industry standard chart of accounts is strategic because it enables the company to better analyze its performance against industry standards and to use benchmarking as a management tool.

In general, the financial planning process for ongoing companies includes both financial planning for the feasibility analysis of new projects and the review and revision of facts, conditions, and strategies for those projects that survived the feasibility analysis and are ongoing. Current project plans are reviewed and modified, and then, integrated with proposed future revenue and expense strategies to create the company's new business plan.

Business plans typically include financial plans that reflect the financial performance of various projects (and/or entities) that represent the entire scope of operations for a particular company. A plan prepared to provide a complete financial analysis of the activities of the company in order to isolate strengths and weaknesses as well as to inform others who must be prepared to defend or help others understand the value of the plan. The plan should demonstrate the company's ability to reduce risks, which is the most valuable skill that an organization can have when it comes to raising capital or planning for survival. It should be a plan prepared to demonstrate the potential return on invested capital and the potential risk to principal, which is an overriding concern for all investors; once investors are comfortable that the principal is relatively secure, they will look for return on investment balanced by the risk inherent in the deal. The strength of any financial plan depends on a conservative expectation of performance. Numerical entries must be conservative; the most probable and meaningful based on direct data, trends, and models. Goals must be achievable using the resources available or which may reasonably be accumulated in the short-term.

Planning documents that are typically incorporated into the financial plan for a homebuilding organization include a Life of Project Projection, Pro-Forma Income Statement, and Cash Flow Projection. These documents are supported by budgets, worksheets, and schedules that would only be made available upon request.

The primary objective of any financial manager is to *maximize the return on invested capital* and financial strategies should focus on this objective first. The best interests of the owners are served by knitting together a number of strategies designed to improve the return on investment, while minimizing unnecessary risks. In most cases, this means strategies and initiatives that will *increase revenue or market share* and *reduce costs* to produce a higher level of profitability. Increasing market share typically results from land, market, and product strategies, and cost reduction strategies involve increasing productivity and operating efficiencies, and eliminating waste.

A ratio is an expression of a mathematical relationship between one quantity and another. Ratios only gain significance when they are compared with: 1) previous ratios of the same company, 2) some predetermined standard, 3) ratios for a benchmark company in the same industry, or 4) standard performance ratios for the industry within which the company operates.

The financial analyst will look for deviations in computed ratios and then look for the causes. In addition to ratio deviations, a financial analyst might also conduct a specific purpose examination, which may include a cash flow, gross margin, break-even, or return on investment analysis. Proper financial analysis employs the use of tools and techniques that examine past and current financial positions to evaluate the potential and future risks associated with a particular company. Such evaluations produce information about trends and relationships, the quality of earnings, and the strengths and weaknesses of a particular company's financial position.

PART II: FINANCING

4 SOURCES OF CAPITAL AND METHODS OF FINANCING   39

5 CONSTRUCTION FINANCING AND THE LOAN PROPOSAL   55

CHAPTER 4

SOURCES OF CAPITAL AND METHODS OF FINANCING

Poor planning is the cause of the vast majority of business failures, and solid financial planning is often the key to long-term success. The capitalization of a company can be complicated and should be evaluated carefully. It should be based on strategies that are consistent with long-term growth and development. Once the business plan has been created, debated, validated, and finalized, it is time to approach capital markets to obtain the funds necessary to support the plan. By this time, the company should be convinced that the plan would produce profits and support its growth and development. The plan should provide the "can do" attitude necessary for the team to move forward; it should help provide the tenacity and determination necessary to persuade others to provide the necessary capital.

The company must remain flexible and willing to alter or revise the plan based on information, opportunities, or limitations developed during the search for capital. The plan should provide the confidence necessary to negotiate a suitable capital position based on targets that have been identified. To establish such targets, the company must know where to look for capital.

CAPITAL REQUIREMENTS

The need for capital arises when new companies incur start-up expenses required to fund operations until revenue from sales is recognized. In growing companies, capital is necessary to fund expanding operations. In many cases, the need for capital can be critical, as in the case of the very successful young company that may be approaching insolvency as a result of growth that has outstripped its ability to obtain the capital necessary for operations; a condition known as "growing a business into bankruptcy." Sources of capital can also be limited as in the case of a small or start-up company that might not have access to public markets or some of the traditional lending sources. These companies often look to friends, relatives, acquaintances, professionals in their sphere of influence, principles of trade contracting companies with whom they do business, and sometimes, venture capitalists, for the investment necessary to secure more conventional financing.

To be successful in highly competitive capital markets, a builder must be willing to extend effort. It takes a high level of determination with a willingness to accept rejection without becoming discouraged. Securing capital is a unique opportunity to build reputation. It is an opportunity to present a professional business plan, which has been validated through the adoption process and ratio analysis, to a group of individuals who understand the importance of being well organized and thoughtful about the direction of a business—a group that understands the value of facts and extraordinary management practice. In most cases, these professionals will be attracted to such presentations of facts that support investment or financial support. To them, it should suggest opportunity. Although they may be limited by their current restrictions or conditions, they will come away with some respect for the builder and his future.

TYPES OF CAPITAL: EQUITY AND DEBT

Every new home builder needs money for start-up to cover general and administrative expenses and to purchase ground, equipment, and material, as well as operating funds to finance land development, construction, receivables, and expansion; without capital, a business cannot be started and an existing business will die. It is out of this need that capital markets have developed and continue to serve the homebuilding industry. There are only two ways to raise money: by sharing ownership or by borrowing. Sharing ownership produces equity capital and borrowing produces *debt capital*. Debt carries a specific repayment obligation while equity is at risk, and any return of or on those funds depends solely on the success of the company. It is this dynamic that creates considerable value for a well-conceived business plan.

The initial capitalization of a closely held building company is often motivated by a dream shared by one or more facilitators with support from family and close friends. Beyond that, raising capital is always a matter of *return on investment* when balanced against *risk*. Two primary advantages of debt capital are that *it does not create a dilution of ownership and interest on debt is tax deductible,* whereas dividends are not. Secured commercial lenders, such as those who provide financing for fixed assets such as trucks, loaders, and model home furniture, or those providing acquisition, development, and construction (ADC) loans that are secured by land and/or improvements, take very little risk and expect modest returns on funds outstanding. Non-secured lenders, by comparison, and equity investors accept the burden of higher risks for a higher return on investment. Generally speaking, the safer the deal, the lower the return on investment, and this is where the business plan becomes central to a lender.

There is a loss of financial flexibility as debt is issued and a firm approaches debt capacity. It is the primary reason for limiting debt and creating a balance between debt and equity; increasing debt also increases the financial risk. Debt should only be used in a way that will serve the best interests of owners or stockholders and maximize their well being. Debt is an amplifier resulting from *leverage* or gearing. It can increase the probability of loss when it is not balanced by equity, and it can provide opportunity when used properly. Risk plays the most important part in determining the balance between debt and equity; where risk is high, debt should be minimal, and the potential for return must drive investment.

EQUITY CAPITAL

Equity capital is an important focus when evaluating a balance sheet for a number of reasons:

◆ It establishes the capacity of the company to undertake financial obligations.

◆ It will determine the company's ability to borrow money at favorable rates.

◆ It provides comfort for both investors and creditors.

◆ It validates the ability of management, and, in publicly held companies.

◆ It is often an indication of the sophistication of management.

Typically, equity financing can be obtained through a private placement with a small number of sophisticated investors, or through a public offering, which is controlled by the United States Securities and Exchange Commission. Often, public offerings result from indirect transfers through investment bankers such as Goldman Sachs, Merrill Lynch, Legg Mason, Solomon Brothers, and Dean Whitter who can help design securities with features that will be most attractive to the market, and then buy the securities from the corporation and resell them to savers or investors. Any attempt to stage a public offering should only be undertaken as a result of professional advice and owners must know that such advice will be expensive. Gap, or equity financing, is usually provided through the sale of stock, a bond issue, or a private investment. Unfortunately, private investment often takes the form of unsecured equity financing with the personal guarantees of the owners.

THE SALE OF STOCK

Although many new homebuilding companies are being established as limited liability companies (LLCs), most large building companies are capitalized through the sale of stock. With a closely held corporation, the stock is purchased by a small number of investors consisting largely of the entrepreneur and his close friends or family, and it is not openly traded on the market. In the case of a public company, the stock is held by a large number of individual, corporate, and institutional investors, and the stock is traded on one of the major stock markets. In most cases, the target for the sale of stock in a home building company is the sophisticated investor; an individual who has a substantial net worth, a substantial income, and can be presumed to understand business and financial statements

COMMON STOCK

The common stockholders are the owners of a company, and the value of their stock will adjust with the performance of the company. They control the voting rights and essentially control the direction and management of the corporation. If the performance of the company is favorable, they may be paid dividends in accordance with company policy. The corporation's primary justification for the issuance of common stock is to reduce risk by creating a basis for ownership and capital investment and to provide a future basis for a capital gain. By comparison, preferred stock carries the obligation of a fixed dividend, but offers no voting rights or voice in company affairs. It is a fictional equity in a sense; it is a hybrid between debt and common stock.

GOING PUBLIC

Going public is expensive and complicated. It should only be an objective of a strategic business decision after very careful consideration. Most offerings are arranged by an investment-banking firm that will act as an underwriter by purchasing all of the initial shares of stock, under certain terms and conditions, and then resell it to the investing public, institutional investors, and other security dealers arranges most offerings. Advanced planning is the key to success and a consultant who has had solid experience in evaluating and negotiating public offerings should guide such an effort. The actual process of selecting an underwriter and then preparing and filing a registration statement with the Securities and Exchange Commission (SEC) is time consuming and can shift the focus of management from the day-to-day operating requirements of the company.

The SEC has explicit standards regarding the financial and non-financial information that must be disclosed in the registration statement and prospectus. In most cases, the investment banker will require the following information:

◆ Brief synopsis of the company including its annual sales and earnings history.

◆ Total amount of funds to be raised, the purpose for raising these funds, and, specifically how the funds will be used.

◆ Detailed explanation of the company and authoritative information about the local and national housing industry and the company's position in that industry. This should include strengths, growth potential, and anything else that sets the company apart from others.

◆ Summary of the *business plan* that the company intends to follow.

◆ Comparative and comprehensive profit and loss statements and balance sheets for three to five years, including the accounting notes.

◆ Opinion of a Certified Public Accountant (CPA) on at least the most recent financial statements.

◆ Product and corporate brochures, as well as recent corporate or site-specific advertising that feature current and proposed production.

This process forces management to become more focused on staff, record keeping, and both strategic and financial planning.

When considering a public offering, the home builder must recognize some key factors that will influence the offering. Some of them include the following:

◆ Historical and future earnings capacity of the company.

◆ Current stock market conditions that will include the general economic outlook, market activity, price/earnings ratios, and activity within the housing industry, to mention a few.

◆ Image of the company in the eyes of investors.

◆ Percentage of additional stock ownership that will be held by the public.

◆ Amount of funds to be raised.

◆ Impact of dilution.

Other factors to consider would be possible incentives for investors. These typically include convertible preferred stock, stock warrants, and stock rights. Convertible preferred stock is stock that can be converted to common stock under certain conditions; warrants are rights to purchase common stock under certain conditions; and, stock rights refer to the rights that are extended to the holders of stock.

PRIVATE INVESTORS

Home builders often prefer private investors to secure the *gap financing* or equity funds required over and above those that are typically provided through the creation of debt. Such funds are necessary to maintain adequate capital reserves and reduce the risk of failure due to inadequate working capital. This source of capitalization allows them to maintain tighter control over their businesses, it avoids the substantial costs related to a public offering, and it eliminates the need for public disclosure. In almost all cases, private investors will focus on:

◆ Potential return on investment for the deal.

◆ Anticipated return on equity for the operating entity as a whole.

◆ Credit worthiness of the entrepreneur or operating entity.

◆ Ability of the company to protect and repay the principal.

◆ Possibility of leveraging a common stock position.

◆ Financial position of the operating entity presented by a compilation or audit.

◆ Financial strength of the individual or individuals where personal guarantees are involved.

◆ Contingent liabilities of the entrepreneur or operating entity.

Private investors are primarily concerned with the protection of principal and will expect the builder or operating entity to have at least as many dollars at risk as the investor. In many cases, they will also expect to receive their distributions of both earnings and principal before the builder.

OTHER SOURCES OF EQUITY CAPITAL

Home builders often use joint ventures, limited partnerships, and limited liability companies (which are all discussed in detail in Chapter 6) to raise substantial amounts of working capital. Although such sources can produce substantial cash assets with limited liability, the ability to use them depends on a track record or a history of outstanding performance.

DEBT CAPITAL

The amount of debt capital available to any particular company is almost solely dependent on the level of equity capital that the company has been able to raise. The degree of leverage proposed becomes one of the most significant elements of a loan application, and builders must be very familiar with the concept. Leverage is a measurement of the percentage of a company's assets that are supported by debt or equity. Leverage ratios are critical and must be considered carefully during the planning process, as well as by potential lenders evaluating a loan application (see Leverage Ratios, Chapter 3). Understanding the concept of leverage is a basic principle of financial management because it enables planners to use leverage to their advantage. Some facts related to leverage include the following:

◆ Increasing leverage usually reduces earnings as a result of the cost related to interest and fees (points) associated with debt.

◆ Increasing leverage usually increases the return on equity; *as will increasing inventory turnover.*

◆ Risk is a natural companion of leverage and must be considered carefully. Liquidity ratios and *accounts payable* are particularly important when considering positions of high leverage.

◆ Some of the criteria used by lenders to compare leverage alternatives include availability, profitability, reliability, flexibility, and risk.

Debt financing is typically classified as short-term, intermediate-term, or long-term and may be either secured or unsecured. For the most part, unsecured debt is limited and only available when the company has an excellent credit rating; a particular asset or class of assets secures debt in most instances.

SHORT-TERM DEBT FINANCING

Short-term debt is typically committed for a period of one year or less and typically includes the following:

◆ Trade credit, which is extended by vendors.

◆ Loans for one year, which are usually made for a specific purpose and are often secured by a receivable or inventory.

◆ Operating lines of credit that may be provided by a lender that will make funds available on a recurring basis up to a given amount. Such loans are typically extended for a renewable one-year period but must be fully paid off for one or more days during that period.

◆ Letters of credit, which are obtained for a fee and facilitate a particular transaction; such letters amount to a conditional bank commitment on behalf of a company, to pay a third party based on specific events and terms. Such instruments are sometimes used for a deposit on the purchase of ground or to guarantee completion of an improvement.

◆ Commercial paper or notes payable that are executed by the company.

INTERMEDIATE-TERM DEBT FINANCING

Intermediate-term debt is committed for a period of less than three years and typically includes the following:

◆ A revolving line of credit, which is a continuing credit line that does not have to be fully paid off at any time; such loans are committed for a specific term with specific restrictions.

◆ Commercial loans such as those related to office equipment, automobiles, trucks, and heavy equipment.

◆ Leases such as those negotiated for office space, office furniture, and model home furniture.

LONG-TERM DEBT FINANCING

Long-term debt is committed for periods of three years or longer and typically includes the following:

◆ Bonds, which are interest-bearing certificates issued by a corporation to raise capital, that promises to pay to the holder, a specific sum on a specified date.

◆ Construction lines of credit, which are borrowing commitments or agreements with a commercial bank that make a specific amount of money available to a borrower on a recurring or revolving basis. Lines of credit typically include a security agreement, which contains conditions and restrictions, rather than a deed of trust.

◆ Mortgage loans, which are notes payable that use real estate as collateral and require periodic payments. They may constitute a first or second trust, depending on their position; a second trust is a debt secured by the same property, but it is junior or subordinate to a first deed of trust.

Mortgage loans include the traditional land acquisition loans, land development loans, and construction loans used by developers and home builders, as well as the consolidated (ADC loans) used by builder/developers, and purchase money mortgages that home builders and developers often use to purchase ground. To be effective, a purchase money mortgage used by a home builder for the acquisition of ground must include a subordination clause, which places it in a second position to a bona fide construction or ADC loan; otherwise, it must be paid off or a specific lot must be released to provide a first trust position for the conventional lender.

Not long ago, the commercial banking industry was composed of more than 10,000 domestically chartered commercial banks that dated back to the 1660s when they were established in the colonies. They were privately owned, subject to taxes, and were primarily focused on lending for commerce and industry. A great deal has changed in the past fifteen years. Today, very large banks that continue to absorb smaller banks control the banking industry.

Long-term debt is a more favorable way for a homebuilding company to broaden its equity base because it eliminates the more frequent cash calls required to pay off short- and intermediate-term debt. Long-term debt provides management flexibility and often establishes the basis for a future public offering by enabling the performance necessary to capture the interest of the public. It is not uncommon for a medium-volume home builder with a strong business plan to negotiate a $3 to $5 million sale in a subordinated debenture offering of 10-year notes using an investment banking firm who would typically place the investments with individual investors all over the country.

The performance of a well-established homebuilding company is largely dependent on local and national cycles of economic expansion and contraction, as well as a variety of local conditions related to the supply of lots, location of projects, competition, and growth policies, to mention a few. The well-managed building company will create carefully conceived business strategies and financial plans, but the accuracy of such plans are most predictable in an 18- to 24-month window. It becomes increasingly difficult to predict sales (the driving force behind all building companies) over the long-term. Investors who have funded long-term debt are more interested in management and performance that consistently returns 25 to 35 percent to justify the perceived risk.

MERGERS AND ACQUISITIONS

Mergers and acquisitions can provide unique opportunities for home builders. When two or more companies are merged, the resulting company can be improved. This maneuver is often made as a method of raising large sums of money, limiting the personal liability of officers and owners, increasing operating efficiencies, and/or preparing to go public. The acquisition of an existing company that is engaged in a similar or supporting activity can sometimes create extraordinary opportunity; it is the primary method of entering new markets for most national home builders.

The motives for such a move can include a desire to enter new markets, obtaining land inventories, improving management capabilities, or, perhaps, a desire on the part of a well-managed company to leverage their position through a turnaround opportunity. It is not uncommon for a homebuilding company to adopt an expansion strategy that targets internal growth as well as with external growth through acquisitions. In still other cases, builders have expanded their operations through vertical integration by acquiring some of the material manufacturers, suppliers, and/or trade contractors that are a significant part of their businesses; they have acquired related companies that support homebuilding activity. Although mergers and acquisitions can be complicated transactions, they should be considered as strategies for growth and development.

SOURCES OF FINANCING

The typical financial package for a home builder includes equity investors, commercial banks, and other asset-based lenders. Companies must choose judiciously among the available financing alternatives, continually monitor their risks and leverage, and carefully guard their sources of finance.

THE PUBLIC

Going public can raise substantial sums of money but it requires management for the benefit of stockholders, subjects the company to substantial costs related to reporting and compliance with the regulations of the Security and Exchange Commission (SEC), and subjects the management to the scrutiny and possible adversary action of stockholders. It will produce the greatest amount of business capital but requires a very lengthy and complex legal process controlled and regulated by the SEC. Typically, it requires at least three years of audited financial data and increased supervision over the company's operations. The first step is to secure an underwriter.

INDIVIDUALS

This is probably the largest source of equity funds for home builders. In addition to friends, relatives, and acquaintances, this group also includes the principles of vendors with whom home builders do business, professionals such as doctors, dentists, and attorneys with disposable income and an interest in investment, foreign investors, and, perhaps clients for whom the builder has constructed a home. This includes a broad group that is only limited by imagination or creative thought.

Since the 1986 tax law revision, individual investors who invest principally in real estate can only offset their passive losses against income from a like source. This makes such investors an attractive opportunity for both debt and equity capital for home builders.

FINANCIAL INSTITUTIONS

Historically, commercial banks and both savings and loan associations and savings banks (the thrifts) have provided more than 90 percent of the acquisition, development, and construction financing for home builders and residential developers. Although most home builders develop long-term relationships with their construction lenders and attempt to establish a *lead lender,* they must recognize that law limits all of these institutions and that the flexibility provided by two or more construction lenders is more realistic in today's financial markets.

As a result of the restructuring by the Federal Government that occurred in the early 90s, there is little difference between the national banks and savings banks of today. There are four regulatory agencies effecting loan limits for this group:

Until recently, the thrift industry included savings and loan associations that were privately owned and established by both federal and state charters, and mutual savings banks that dated back to the 1800s when they were chartered by the states to promote personal savings. Today, the mutual savings banks have disappeared and the industry is consolidating to produce larger savings banks.

Federal Reserve Board (the Fed), which regulates state member banks and bank holding companies.

Federal Deposit Insurance Corporation (FDIC), which insures the deposits of both the banks and the thrifts.

Comptroller of the Currency (OCC), which regulates national banks.

Office of Thrift Supervision (OTS), which regulates federal savings and loan associations and savings banks.

Many believe that this redundancy will lead to an eventual consolidation of both the banking and thrift industries.

COMMERCIAL FINANCE COMPANIES

This includes a small group of asset-based lenders that require a first position on all hard assets, a first or second position on working capital assets, depending on whether a bank has an operating line, and they usually require personal endorsements. Companies like General Electric, Westinghouse, and Heller Financial have long invested in real estate. These companies are becoming a recognized source for both construction and operating funds.

LIFE INSURANCE COMPANIES

Traditionally, life insurance companies (LICs) have not been a major source for residential construction loans; they have opted for the higher-volume commercial projects with higher yields. These companies are state chartered and may be mutually or privately owned. Life insurance companies will invest or lend funds that they receive in the form of premiums for life insurance, annuities, and income from investments. Such loans are made based on a cash-flow projection of benefits predicted by mortality tables, as well as policy. For some years, a number of experts have predicted that these companies will play a larger role in the financing of new home construction, but this has not materialized. In periods when opportunities for commercial investment are diminished by soft markets, LICs may look to large residential developments to fill the gap. Life insurance companies currently hold a substantial portion of the outstanding mortgage-backed securities that support the secondary mortgage market; a market consisting of federal credit agencies, like Fannie Mae and Freddie Mac, and mortgage pools that are available to banks and mortgage brokers for the purchase of loans that are packaged, warehoused, and then sold to others.

PENSION FUNDS

Pension funds consist of both public and private funds that, together, represent a significant potential source for real estate debt financing. State statutes control private funds and Federal statutes control the public funds. While public funds have historically invested in mortgages largely as a matter of political consideration, the private funds have been more attracted by yields and risk levels outside of the housing industry. These funds have significant assets and many believe that they are developing a desire to use real estate to create variety in their investment portfolios. The participation of private pension funds in the housing industry will depend largely on the industry's ability to compete with other alternatives.

REAL ESTATE INVESTMENT TRUSTS

A real estate investment trust (REIT) is a tax-exempt corporation that raises capital for real estate ventures by selling stock or commercial paper. It passes 90 percent of its revenue through to shareholders; there must be more than 100 stockholders with no fewer than six owning 50 percent or more of the trust as a group. More than 75 percent of their assets and income must be real estate-related. Some experts anticipate that pension funds will invest in REITs that have been created for investment in single-family projects to diversify risks and generate higher yields.

Real estate investment trusts are a good source for equity capital; they serve as a vehicle for investors to take equity positions in a range of real estate projects. In the future, these trusts will probably become a key source for unregulated, single-family construction funds, but the costs of such financing may be substantial.

INVESTMENT BANKS AND VENTURE CAPITAL FIRMS

Venture capital is a primary source of financing for new or expanding companies considered too risky by banks or other traditional lenders; venture capital is considered risk money that often permits a small business to grow and develop. Such financing may be obtained from an individual, a group of individuals, or one or more institutional investors, for a share of the profits or a very high return on investment. Venture capital is always easier to obtain when a company plans to eventually go public.

There are four basic methods of obtaining this high risk capital from investment banks or venture capitalists.

Common Stock
An issue of common stock includes representation on the board as well as other controls that will ensure adequate performance.

Preferred Stock
An issue of preferred stock will usually include dividends (often 6 to 8 percent), a repurchase agreement to insure return on investment, and/or a provision for a conversion (convertible preferred stock) to common stock.

Convertible Debenture
Convertible debenture is a loan that may be converted to common stock, in which case, the conversion price, the interest rate, and the conditions are all negotiated.

A Loan with Warrants
A loan with warrants is a loan that includes a detachable stock option; even if the loan is paid off, the investor would still have the option to buy stock.

Investment banks represent public and private operating companies, wealthy individual investors, private trusts, and entrepreneurs, and they typically grow out of venture capital firms, securities brokerage houses, or small consulting firms. They act as financial advisors, they will act as an underwriter for an initial public stock offering (IPO), they will buy and sell operating companies for their own account, and they will finance deals from their own resources.

Venture capital firms will only back strong management by providing equity, mezzanine, and sometimes secured financing for start-up or first or second stage developing companies. The quality of the individual entrepreneur, which includes maturity, experience, and track record, is one of the primary focuses of the venture capitalist looking for return on investment. They are interested in a fixed return but prefer to take an equity position in either a public offering or net income, and they may expect very high, exorbitant, or even unreasonable returns on their investment. Venture capital typically falls into one of the following categories:

◆ Start-up or first-round financing; this is the most difficult to obtain, but amounts to almost one-third of all such financing.

◆ Development stage or second-round financing; this type of financing is only required after some history has been established.

◆ Expansion stage or third-round financing.

◆ Growth stage or fourth-round financing.

◆ Leveraged buy-out, which occurs when a team of skilled managers purchases an existing company, and the sale is structured and brokered by the venture capital company.

◆ Turnaround opportunity where the venture capitalist finances and provides management for a troubled or bankrupt business.

◆ Public offering resulting from a venture capital company or venturesome mutual fund having bought the equity in a new issue or second-round public offering for a business on a path of high-growth potential.

Venture capital firms make loans with slightly more risks than those associated with bank loans where the risk of loss is almost negligible. For this reason, the venture capitalist will become more involved in your business. Venture capital companies include:

Public Companies
These are companies that are traded on the various stock exchanges.

Private Companies
Private companies are those often founded by pension funds and insurance companies.

Bank-Related Companies
These are companies that have been established by a number of large money center banks to circumvent the laws that prevent them from owning stock in small businesses.

Large Corporate Venture Companies
Large corporate venture companies have been established by major U.S. corporations as subsidiaries or as major investors in one or more venture capital pools.

MORTGAGE BANKERS

Mortgage bankers are subject to state and corporate laws in the state or states where they operate. Most are members of the Mortgage Bankers Association, and they act as temporary brokers between borrowers and investors. Typically, they will obtain a commitment from an investor, originate the loans, sell the loans back to the investor, and retain the servicing for a fee; they sell all of the mortgages that they originate and, therefore, hold very little mortgage debt.

At one time, home builders used mortgage bankers to secure permanent financing for their purchasers; take-out commitments were often required by construction lenders to ensure that an adequate supply of permanent financing would be available for purchasers as houses were completed. Today, however, permanent financing is plentiful, and the role of the mortgage banker has changed. Home builders will sometimes use mortgage bankers to act as agents or originators of construction financing for specific projects. Although they do not typically engage in construction lending, they may help place such loans in their network through conduit affiliates. In such cases, the mortgage banker typically receives a commission or origination fee for securing the required financing for a builder.

OTHER SOURCES

Foreign investors have traditionally provided some construction money for residential construction in selected markets. These sources of financing have been predominantly limited to larger homebuilding and land development companies, and only after a great deal of "due diligence" in the form of very formal financing applications with considerable information resulting from careful study. Some home builders with experience managing foreign investors find that the need for continuous contact and demands for detailed operating information can become a serious burden.

Other corporations are sometimes suitable sources for either debt of equity capital for home builders. It would not be unusual for a developer or major trade contractor to maintain a financial interest in a homebuilding company through corporate investment. This is an opportunity that is probably underutilized by most home builders.

CHAPTER SUMMARY

There are only two ways to raise money: by *sharing ownership* or by *borrowing*. Sharing ownership produces *equity capital* and borrowing produces *debt capital*.

Raising capital is always a matter of *return on investment* when balanced against *risk*. Two primary advantages of debt capital are that it does not create a dilution of ownership and interest on debt is tax deductible, while dividends are not.

There is a loss of financial flexibility as debt is issued and a firm approaches debt capacity. It is the primary reason for limiting debt and creating a balance between debt and equity; this increases the financial risk.

Debt is an amplifier resulting from *leverage*. It can increase the probability of loss where it is not balanced by equity and it can provide opportunity where it is used properly. Risk plays the most important part in determining the balance between debt and equity; where risk is high, debt should be minimal and the potential for return must drive investment.

Equity capital is an important focus when evaluating a balance sheet for a number of reasons: (1) it establishes the capacity of the company to undertake financial obligations, (2) it will determine the company's ability to borrow money at favorable rates, (3) it provides comfort for both investors and creditors, (4) it validates the ability of management, and, in publicly held companies, (5) it is often an indication of the sophistication of management.

With a *closely held* corporation, the stock is purchased by a small number of investors consisting largely of the entrepreneur and his close friends or family, and it is not openly traded on the market. In the case of a *public* company the stock is held by a large number of individual, corporate, and institutional investors and the stock is traded on one of the major stock markets.

Leverage is a measurement of the percentage of a company's assets that are supported by debt or equity. Leverage ratios are critical and must be considered carefully during the planning process; as will potential lenders following a loan application.

Some facts related to leverage include the following:

1. Increasing leverage reduces earnings as a result of the cost related to interest and fees (points) associated with debt
2. Increasing leverage will generally increase the return on equity; *as will increasing inventory turnover*
3. Risk is a natural companion of leverage and must be considered carefully. Liquidity ratios and *accounts payable* are particularly important when considering positions of high leverage
4. Some of the criteria used by lenders to compare leverage alternatives include availability, profitability, reliability, flexibility, and risk

Debt financing is typically classified as short-term, intermediate-term, or long-term and may be either secured or unsecured.

Historically, commercial banks and both savings and loan associations and savings banks (the thrifts) have provided more than 90 percent of the acquisition, development, and construction financing for home builders and residential developers.

Venture capital is a primary source of financing for new or expanding companies considered too risky by banks or other traditional lenders. There are four basic methods of obtaining this high risk capital from investment banks or venture capitalists:

Common Stock—an issue of common stock, which generally will include representation on the board as well as other controls that will insure adequate performance
Preferred Stock—an issue of preferred stock, which generally will include dividends (often 6 to 8 percent), a repurchase agreement to insure return on investment, and/or a provision for a conversion (convertible preferred stock) to common stock
Convertible Debenture—a loan to the company that may be converted to common stock in which case, the conversion price, the interest rate, and the conditions are all negotiated.
A Loan with Warrants—a loan to the company that includes a detachable stock option; if the loan is paid off they still have the option to buy stock

The typical financial package for a builder includes equity investors, commercial banks, and other asset-based lenders. Companies must choose judiciously among the available financing alternatives, continually monitor their risks and leverage, and carefully guard their sources of finance.

CHAPTER 5

CONSTRUCTION FINANCING AND THE LOAN PROPOSAL

Home builders need to be flexible in their thinking about construction financing. They need to take advantage of whatever sources they feel are open to them, and they should settle on the loan that offers the best rate and terms available at the time. The days of relationship banking are essentially over and while builders must maintain healthy relationships with their lenders and the senior officers that service their account, they must recognize the importance of shopping loans. Their loans will be more strictly evaluated based on financial standards and performance, and will have much less to do with the strength of relationships.

There are a number of options available to builders and land developers when it comes to financing their projects. Developers typically negotiate loans for acquisition and development. Home builders typically use a construction loan with a land advance in order to buy and build on a finished lot. The builder/developer will typically negotiate an ADC loan: a loan with a land advance, a development draw schedule, and a construction draw schedule. These loans can be negotiated for the development of a single parcel, a new home subdivision, or a single home on a finished lot. Or, as in many other instances, builders and developers may negotiate a line of credit to cover development and/or construction. Each loan must be tailored to meet the needs of both the borrower and the lender and the market forces of supply and demand will affect each loan. Borrowers must evaluate the financing options that are available and decide which options make the most sense.

In recent years, a large number of home builders with land inventories have discovered the advantages of a combined construction and permanent loan, known as a *construction/perm loan*. These loans are made directly to the homebuyer based on his credit position; regulators consider these loans consumer loans and they may even have a higher loan-to-value ratio than a conventional construction loan. The home builder sells and closes the lot to the homebuyer, and then completes the construction under a contract with a draw schedule funded by the bank. This type of financing works well for the builder because it eliminates the origination fee that would be paid on a construction loan, it does not tie up the builder's credit, and it generally produces some income on the sale of the lot. It works well for the purchaser because it avoids a double settlement, one on the construction loan with the builder and one on the permanent loan with the buyer, while insuring that the builder he has chosen will build the house at a fixed price.

CONSTRUCTION LENDING

Historically, commercial banks and thrifts have provided most of the financing required for the homebuilding industry. Although the changes that occurred in the savings industry in the early 1990s have generally reduced the activity of the thrifts in construction lending, they remain a significant source of funds for home builders. In a recent study conducted by the National Association of Home Builders, approximately 87 percent of all home builders indicated that they relied on commercial banks and/or thrifts for financing; 75 percent used commercial banks and almost 12 percent used thrifts. For this reason, the detailed discussion of acquisition, development, and construction financing will be limited to those loans typically placed with banks and thrifts.

When dealing with institutional lenders such as commercial banks and thrifts, it is important to understand their limitations and requirements. Banks and thrifts are limited in the amount of funds that they can lend to one borrower, they are limited by maximum loan to value ratios, they must meet risk-based capital requirements, and they themselves can further limit the amount of funds that they are willing to lend or advance on a draw schedule. Builders must analyze their loan submissions and be certain that they do not exceed the standard loan limitations or requirements established either by statute or bank policy.

Loan Limitations
The total loans to one borrower may not exceed 15 percent of the institutions unimpaired capital, with the exception that an additional 10 percent may be advanced if that amount is fully secured by marketable collateral. This is probably a good argument for larger banks and thrifts.

Loan-to-Value (LTV)
There are guidelines for banks and thrifts that restrict the amount of funds that they can advance for specific purposes. These restrictions are known as maximum loan-to-value ratios and they are as follows:

◆ Loans or advances on raw ground are limited to 65 percent of the appraised value.

◆ Land development loans or land and advances are limited to 75 percent of the improved lot value.

◆ Construction loans or finished land and advances on single-family (1 to 4 family residential construction) housing are limited to 85 percent of the appraised value at completion although most lenders will not lend more than 80 percent.

In the case of an ADC loan, the advances for each phase would be restricted by the above listed loan-to-value restrictions. That is to say that the total land advance would be limited to 65 percent of the appraised raw lot value; the development advances would be limited to 75 percent of the appraised finished lot value less the funds advanced on the raw lot; and, the total construction advances would be restricted to 85 percent of the appraised value of the finished home (on a finished lot) less the total funds advanced for the land and development. It is easy to see that the appraisal report on such loans can become a significant concern for a borrower and will sometimes alter the lender's ability to make the loan under the terms anticipated by the borrower.

Risk-Based Capital Requirements

Banks and thrifts must meet risk-based capital requirements or capital reserves based on the types of loans that they make. They must reserve $8.00 in capital for every $100 in assets. For these purposes, loans are weighted based on risks; a 50 percent risk weight is assigned for single-family home mortgages and a 100 percent risk weight is assigned for construction and land development loans. This means that in the event that the institution advanced $300,000 in a construction loan, they would be required to maintain a capital reserve of $24,000, as opposed to a $12,000 reserve for the same dollars in a home mortgage.

Draw Schedules

These are summaries of disbursements that are proposed or established for the advancement of funds under a development or construction loan. In some cases, they are proposed by the builder or developer and approved by the lender, in some cases they are established by policy, and in still others, they are the result of a negotiation between the lender and borrower. In theory, the funds advanced, should have some relationship to the cost of construction or development that has been paid as work progresses; the value of the property is generally improved based on the value added by the work in process. These schedules for construction loans can be simple seven-stage draw schedules or, perhaps, more complicated ten- or twelve-stage draw schedules. In any case, the stages should clearly specify the activities that are to be complete at each stage. A typical seven-stage construction draw schedule generally might include the following activity completion requirements:

◆ **Foundation**—clearing; excavation; footings and foundation walls; plumbing groundwork; under slab radon and drainage, damp proofing, and soil poison; and, basement and garage slabs complete   (15%)

◆ **Second Deck**—sewer and water connections; foundation backfill and rough grading; first-floor deck and wall framing; and, second deck complete   (10%)

◆ **Under Roof**—second floor wall and roof framing; windows, exterior doors, and stairs set; and, the roof papered in   (15%)

◆ **Ready Drywall**—mechanical, plumbing, and electrical rough-ins complete; air stopping and insulation complete; roof shingle complete; exterior trim complete; brick or stone veneer complete; and, siding complete   (25%)

◆ **Drywall Complete**—drywall hung, taped, blocked, finished, and sanded; and, exterior painting complete   (10%)

◆ **Interior Trim**—interior doors set; interior trim complete; ceramic baths complete; cabinets and vanities set; and, exterior walks and drive complete   (15%)

◆ **Final**—interior paint; appliances set; mechanical, plumbing, and electrical finals; floors finished; hardware installed; and, landscaping complete   (10%)

In most instances, the lender will require a title rundown before the disbursement of any draw, in order to be certain that no mechanic's liens have been filed since the last disbursement. Final draws are usually held to 10 percent and are seldom drawn when a house is pre-sold and the purchaser is waiting for settlement; in those cases, the closing or settlement is coordinated to coincide with completion of the house and the total loan, less the final draw, is repaid at settlement.

A TYPICAL CONSTRUCTION LOAN WITH A LAND ADVANCE

The Facts

The ABC Building Company, Inc. has contracted to purchase a finished lot in a new subdivision from a local land developer. The contract price for the lot is $95,000 cash at settlement and the company plans to build a house on speculation that will sell for $370,000. The bank has had the lot and improvements appraised, approved the loan, and issued a commitment.

The Loan Summary

Total Loan Amount (LTV ratio of 80%)			$296,000
Funds are to be disbursed as follows:			
Land Advance at settlement (LTV ration of 75%)			$71,250
Balance in seven draws as follows:			$224,750
	1st Draw	15%	$ 33,700
	2nd Draw	10%	$ 22,470
	3rd Draw	15%	$ 36,500
	4th Draw	25%	$ 56,180
	5th Draw	10%	$ 22,470
	6th Draw	15%	$ 33,700
	7th Draw	10%	$ 22,530
Rate		1.5% over prime	
Term		18 months	
Fee		1.5% (one and one half point)	

In the loan example set forth in above figure, the builder would require the following approximate cash to settle both the land contract and the loan:

Cash above the loan for the ground (25% of purchase price)	$ 23,750
Loan Fee (1.5%)	4,440
Approximate Attorney's Fees and Settlement Charges	8,000
Total Approximate Cash Requirement	$ 36,190

Keep in mind that the builder has borrowed 80 percent of the total value of the lot and improvements. This means that if the builder were estimating a 10 percent net margin and a 3 percent sales commission to be *paid at closing,* the out-of-pocket cash requirement to fund the construction to completion would be 7 percent of the sales price (80%+7%+3%+10%=100%). In the example, the difference between the cash required to close the lot and loan ($36,190) and the cash required to cover costs ($25,900 @7%), would be residual cash ($10,290) that would be recovered by the builder as funds are disbursed by the lender. It is this dynamic that often confuses new home builders and results in "checkbook management." Cash flow must not be confused with profits, which are typically only recognized at the end of the year. It takes a substantial amount of equity funds to properly manage a homebuilding company and this generally means large cash reserves if the company is managed properly.

PARTICIPATION LOANS

Lenders have the ability to engage in *participation loans.* In such cases, two or more lenders will agree to fund a loan based on percentages of participation and the originating lender will generally service the loan for the participants. Participation lending will help lenders make larger loans where loan limitations to one borrower might otherwise be a problem, or it may simply be a case where they want to accommodate a borrower but wish to lay off a portion of the risk.

A REVOLVER

A *revolver* is a provision in an ADC loan that allows the borrower to draw the construction funds down, pay them back, and then draw them down again. As a result of the revolver provision, the total loan is lower than would be required with a conventional loan.

A TYPICAL ADC LOAN FOR A NEW HOME SUBDIVISION WITH A REVOLVER PROVISION

The Facts

The ABC Building Company, Inc. has contracted to purchase a 10-acre parcel that has been fully approved for 40 single-family detached building lots. The land contract provides for a purchase price of $40,000 per lot, or a total price of $1,600,000. The seller of the land has agreed to take back a purchase money mortgage in the amount of $160,000, or $4,000 per lot, with a rate of 5% for a term of 30 months. The Company will develop the ground and build the houses. The development costs are expected to be $47,000 per lot, or $1,880,000 and the homes will be built from three models with an average sales price of $370,000. The Company estimates that they will not have more than twenty (20) units under construction at any one time. The bank has had the property and improvements appraised, approved the loan with a revolver provision, and issued a commitment.

The Loan Summary	Max Per/Unit	Total
Total Loan Amount (LTV ratio of 80%)	$296,000	$7,225,000
Funds are to be disbursed as follows:		
Acquisition Funds at settlement (LTV ratio of 65%)	$ 26,000	$1,040,000

Development Funds ($87,000×.75–$26,000) $ 39,250 $1,570,000
    As work progresses at 90% of costs
Construction Funds (20 units maximum at $230,750 $4,615,000
  any one time)

        In draws at work progresses

1st Draw	(15%)	$ 34,600	
2nd Draw	(10%)	$ 23,100	
3rd Draw	(15%)	$ 34,600	
4th Draw	(25%)	$ 57,650	
5th Draw	(10%)	$ 23,100	
6th Draw	(15%)	$ 34,600	
7th Draw	(10%)	$ 23,100	

Rate: 1% over prime
Term: 30 months
Fee: 1% (one point)
Construction loan without the provision.

Revolvers are particularly effective on larger projects, where loan limitations might otherwise be restrictive and they are less expensive to the builder; the origination fee on such loans is based on the total loan limit.

The total loan limit is determined by the total number of units that may be under construction at any one time. This is the key to determining the maximum loan amount and it is critical that builders determine this number carefully. In the example below, the builder has determined that there will be no more than twenty units under construction at any one time. This established the total construction funds required; when added to the acquisition and development portions of the loan, the total construction funds required for the twenty units determines the total loan limit. As homes are closed, curtailments would be made and thereby make room for new starts.

In the above ADC financing example, the company only pays the origination fee on the total funds it expects use as a result of the revolver; in this case, the fee will be calculated on the total loan amount of $7,225,000 as opposed to a loan amount of $11,840,000 which would be the total for an ADC loan without the revolver provision. The builder would require the following approximate cash to settle both the land and the loan:

Cash above the loan to settle the ground (25% of purchase price) $ 400,000
Loan Fee (one point or 1%) $ 72,250
Approximate Attorney's Fees and Settlement Charges $ 25,000
Total Approximate Cash Required $ 497,250

INTEREST RESERVES AND OTHER SET-ASIDES

Some construction lenders may require an interest reserve. By placing funds in an escrow account from which interest payments can be made, the lender insures against a short-term default resulting from a failure to keep interest payments current. Set asides can also be used for the payment of other obligations that may be of concern to the lender. Although such provisions are rare in cases where the home builder is experienced with a credible track record, they are sometimes used.

CONSTRUCTION LINES OF CREDIT

This form of construction lending is a departure from the traditional financing that is secured by a particular lot or parcel of property. It is a loan that permits the borrower to draw funds, up to a certain limit, as work progresses, pay the loan down as cash-flow permits, and then to draw the funds again over a specified period of time. Such lines of credit are negotiated with large institutional lenders, or a pool of lenders, and are typically secured by the assets of the company based on a security agreement. A fee is generally paid to reserve the funds and interest is paid on the funds outstanding monthly.

When a builder's personal net worth is substantial, he or she may be able to limit potential liability to a fixed amount and thereby protect a portion of his or her personal wealth. Such limited liability endorsements should be reviewed and approved by an attorney in order to insure that the intent of the limited endorsement is clear. For most home builders, the only way to avoid personal endorsement is to become a public company.

This form of financing is preferred by many large companies in lieu of conventional construction loans because it is less expensive and eliminates the ongoing requirement to settle and release construction loan deeds of trust, which is both costly and time consuming. Lenders using a construction line of credit are generally not as well protected from the effects of potential liens and judgments, and it is, therefore, critical to the lender that the quality of management is consistently high and that the company's debt-to-equity ratio is low; in most cases, such lines are only available to companies with significant retained earnings and an excellent track record.

THE LOAN PROPOSAL

The business plan is the anchor for any financing proposal. The proposed financing must be evaluated in terms of its relationship to the objectives of that business plan. As a home builder organization grows and develops, it is not necessary, nor is it always desirable, to disclose the strategies and financial implications for an entire company or its business plan when a single project loan is the objective. The loan proposal should be tailored for the financing need. It may not be necessary to share the entire plan. In such cases, the builder might submit a loan proposal with strategies and a financial plan for the specific project only. The submission would typically include the material described in the previous chapter, to include current financial statements for the company, and also, perhaps, the individual who will endorse the loan (see Appendix B).

Like the business plan, creating a loan proposal is a dynamic and interactive process. It is an accumulation of both assumptions and projections and will, in large part, determine the success or failure of the project. If the proposal is presented in a clear and readable form, it will not only convey the company's goals and methods of attaining those goals, but it will also capture a reviewer's attention. Like a business plan, a well-conceived loan proposal that is supported by facts, data, studies, and the like will do more to marshal support and provide investors, lenders, employees, and others good reason for aggressively supporting the proposal

THE LENDING PROCESS

The lending process is that series of considerations or actions that are necessary for a borrower to initiate a loan and for a lender to process the loan application, gain approval, and issue a commitment. It includes everything that occurs from the time that the loan is initiated to the time it is closes.

INITIATING THE LOAN

Initiating the loan really consists of a series of preparatory activities that a borrower must follow in order to improve the probability of success. These activities consist of prospecting, qualifying the source, controlling the approach, presenting the plan, and handling objections or areas of concern. Each phase requires some thought or action as follows:

Prospecting
Prospecting is the process of looking for the right investors and lenders. A borrower must examine the alternatives, target potential lenders and investors carefully, and not disclose the business plan or proposal to anyone without a purpose.

Qualifying the Source
Before settling on the lending targets, the borrower must first understand who they are and what their capacities are. What are their total assets and how will that limit their loans to one borrower? Do they have a record of participation lending or do they have the ability to obtain a participating lender? What is their track record for construction and/or development loans? Do other builders hold them in high regard? Aside from the fees and interest, why would they be interested in developing a relationship?

Controlling the Approach
Target the lender, work from above with senior officers wherever possible, identify the loan officer, and develop an effective approach. Use whatever network you can and avoid getting too detailed in casual meetings that have not been scheduled for the purpose of presentation.

Presenting the Plan
The key to financing is adequate preparation and determination. The proposal must be a well-conceived strategic and financial plan, presented with enthusiasm and a determination to give it life; disappointments must not discourage or diminish the energy necessary to foster a dream. Some lenders will ask to see the proposal with the intention of becoming involved, while others may be more curious about the borrower's capacities, the terms of the deal, or they may become unreasonable in their demands; a bright man once said that financing a project can sometimes be like finding the right foot for Cinderella's slipper. A borrower looking for financing must be patient, flexible, and persistent.

Handling Objections or Areas of Concern
A good plan will consider the negatives; it will present comparisons, consider the impact of failure, and identify the deep pockets or those who will carry the greatest bur-

den of risk. Keep in mind that management is the most important feature of any plan. Understand the plan and be prepared to defend it.

LOAN APPLICATION

An application for a construction loan should be a very formal and professional presentation, containing a detailed loan proposal prepared by the builder that, as a minimum, includes the following:

◆ A **cover letter** outlining the proposal that includes the borrowing entity, the timing, and the status of architectural and engineering plans.

◆ An **area map** locating the site.

◆ A **locator map** showing the site and adjacent areas with an emphasis on the approach conditions.

◆ A number of **pictures** of the site showing its basic character and topography.

◆ A copy of the **land contract** with all exhibits, attachments, and addenda.

◆ A complete **market study** including a map showing significant competition; this study should include demographics, a survey of competition, and an analysis of competing projects both in process and in planning.

◆ Both a **project and cash budget** (cash-flow analysis).

◆ A **financing summary** that includes the loan amount, proposed terms and conditions of the loan, a disclosure of the sources and amount of equity investment, and a listing of any proposed guarantors.

◆ A summary of **background information** including a company resume, company financial statements, and the financial statements of any proposed guarantors.

◆ Copies of relevant **engineering and architectural plans,** including a copy of the site plan and record plat (if available) and copies of architectural plans for each proposed structure.

UNDERWRITING

Construction loan underwriting is based on an appraisal of the property, the company's ability to complete the project based on historical performance, its demonstration of financial responsibility, its financial ability to carry the project in the event of an unforeseen problem, and the financial strength of the guarantors. It is the process of evaluating the financial risks related to a loan based on established standards. Such risks can often be reduced by lenders through participation, purchasing insurance, requiring additional security, or modifying the proposed terms and conditions. Often this is necessary in order to establish an exposure that is well-balanced and permits a loan committee to accept the financial responsibility for the loan. In general, underwriters look for what is known as the four Cs of lending:

◆ Character

◆ Cash flow

◆ Collateral

◆ Contribution

The Appraisal

Technically, appraisals are unbiased estimates of the nature, quality, value, or utility of an interest in specific real estate; they can be either an evaluation or a valuation. In most cases, appraisals are based on a process of estimating fair market value, investment value, or insurable value of a specific property as of a particular date. For lending purposes, appraisals are used to establish current fair-market value of real estate and they are part of the underwriting process.

The current fair-market value is based on current market conditions and the future benefits of acquisition. There are three basic approached used by an appraiser to establish current fair market value:

◆ The sales comparison approach, which established value based on a comparison of recent sales of comparable properties.

◆ The cost approach, which establishes value based on a determination of the value of the land, plus the cost of reproducing or replacing improvements, less the loss in value due to depreciation.

$$value = value\ of\ land + cost\ of\ improvements - depreciation$$

◆ The income capitalization approach, which establishes value determined by the earnings potential of the property based on a capitalization of income.

$$value = income \div capitalization\ rate)$$

Where the appraiser calculates the income approach, the capitalization rate is the result of the anticipated rate of return for a specific investor group (yield rate) and the annualized component that allows for a return of capital.

An individual who has been trained and is certified in the appraisal process generally prepares an appraisal report; they are professionals who are qualified to make judgments about real estate values based on accepted appraisal practices. In most instances, the lender will select the appraiser, the appraisal will be ordered by the bank, and the appraisal report will be submitted to the bank. The borrower typically pays for the report and a copy is often made available to the borrower upon request.

Contingent Liability

The liability created by development and construction loans is generally substantial and it includes both corporate and personal liabilities in most cases. This liability is the focus of underwriters. Contingent liability is a classification of obligations that are created by an owner as he or she endorses leases, guarantees loans or lines of credit, and guarantees performance by endorsing performance and payment bonds, as well as warranty agreements. Most home builders and land developers assume considerable contingent liability as a result of their operations and this liability is not so obvious. In some cases, underwriters will want to know the terms and conditions of existing debt and guarantees, and will sometimes ask for a schedule. Some forms of contingent personal liability result from guarantees required on the following:

◆ Acquisition, development, and construction loans.

◆ Construction lines of credit.

◆ Commercial loans and credit lines.

◆ Invested capital.

◆ Long-term leases for offices or equipment.

◆ Accounts with major suppliers.

◆ Payment and performance bonds.

◆ Home warrantee programs.

◆ Municipal improvement agreements, sometimes known as public improvement agreements and site plan enforcement agreements.

Lender relationships are critical once a loan has been closed. Keeping the lender informed is the best policy. In the event of a crisis, never keep secrets from your lender. Rather evaluate the circumstances, obtain help from a consultant if necessary, and be prepared to present solutions. Borrowers must lead their companies and lenders through a crisis, but lenders can be very resourceful when they are committed to providing help.

Although home builders may be organized as a corporation for the purposes of limiting personal liability, such contingent liability can be substantial.

THE LOAN COMMITTEE

The final review and approval of a construction loan request will be the result of an action taken by a loan committee. Loan committees are typically composed of senior officers of the bank, board members, and/or advisors. Loans are typically presented to the committee by the originator or a senior officer of the bank.

THE COMMITMENT

Following the approval of a loan request, the lender will provide the builder with a written loan commitment that outlines the basic business provisions of the loan. This is typically, a summary letter of the business points that will be covered in detail in the legal documents that will follow. The commitment letter must be read carefully and any concerns or points requiring clarification should be discussed and resolved prior to the preparation of the final loan document. Commitment letters generally require that the borrower sign and return a copy, demonstrating a clear understanding of what will follow. In some cases, they require a fee that must be paid before the lender will process the final loan documents required for settlement.

Some of the most important information set forth in the loan commitment includes, the loan amount and disbursement schedule, the interest rate and fees to be paid, the term of the loan and a provision for an extension, any requirement for personal endorsement, and critical dates.

CLOSING THE LOAN

The loan closing, or settlement, is a formal process typically conducted by a real estate attorney for the purpose of completing the loan transaction, recording the resulting documents, and disbursing some of the funds. Often, such closings occur simultaneously with the settlement of a land contract for the ground required for the project. The actual loan documents, which are generally provided by the lender's attorney in preparation for the loan closing may include:

◆ A building and loan agreement, provides the detailed terms and conditions of the loan along with appropriate draw schedules.

◆ A guarantee agreement, which generally provides personal and corporate guarantees for the repayment of the debt.

◆ The note, serves as evidence of the debt;.

◆ The deed of trust, is recorded in the land records and establishes the security for the loan.

Understanding the building and loan agreement is critical to maintaining a healthy relationship with the construction lender.

The building and loan agreement is a formal legal document and it is critical because it sets forth the terms and conditions of the loan. These conditions must be clearly understood prior to execution by a borrower. In addition to defining the conditions of default, this document will contain other critical information relative to the loan. A failure to build or develop in accordance with plans and specifications, or to pay the interest and fees when due, typically constitutes a default, which almost always accelerates the loan and requires payment in full. The building and loan agreement may require cross-collateralization of particular assets or contain a cross-default provision. Cross-collateralization would be a requirement to secure the debt with assets that are not part of the loan; this is often an unreasonable request because builders typically use separate entities for each project and they are often financed by other lenders. A *cross default* provision generally states that *a* default on any other construction or development loan would constitute a default under the new loan; this would create a very serious condition for a builder that inadvertently commits a technical default (perhaps resulting from some relatively minor variations from the plans or specifications), or experiences financial distress on a project totally unrelated to the subject loan. Each provision of a building and loan agreement must be analyzed carefully and understood by the builder prior to execution. If there are serious questions, consult an attorney.

In addition to attorney's fees for settling the loan, builders are also generally responsible for the preparation of documents, title insurance, recordation charges, and miscellaneous settlement expenses. In some cases, particularly where a new building company is the borrower, the lender may also require a completion bond, which guarantees the completion of construction. Such bonds are often available from major material suppliers, based on the builder's relationship and a commitment for future business.

THE PURCHASE-MONEY MORTGAGE

A purchase-money trust or mortgage, or "seller take-back financing" as it is sometimes referred to, is an excellent method of reducing the cash requirements necessary to fund a land deal. With this condition of sale, the seller agrees to take back a note in lieu of cash for a portion of the land purchase price. The terms and conditions of such financing can vary considerably, but generally reflect the willingness of a landowner to share some of the risks associated with land development and/or construction. Most such trusts provide for:

◆ A term that approximates the life of the project and sometimes has an automatic short-term extension built in.

◆ A rate of interest that is two or three points over prime, which is generally considered an inducement for the note holder to make the loan.

◆ The personal endorsement of builder, or at least one officer of a building company.

◆ Will often provide for accelerated releases, in which case the purchaser would be required to pay five or ten percent more than pro-rata (the total debt divided by the number of parcels, sections, or lots) for the release of a parcel, section, or lot.

THE SUBORDINATED PURCHASE-MONEY MORTGAGE

A subordinated purchase-money mortgage is seller take-back financing that is in a second trust position to a bona fide acquisition, development, and/or construction loan. In the ADC loan, the purchaser reduces the cash required at settlement by $320,000.

With the subordinated purchase-money mortgage, the land seller is providing financing that is in a "second position" to the ADC lender. That is, in the event of a default under the acquisition, development, and/or construction loan or, in the case of bankruptcy, the lender would be in a senior position and therefore, be paid out before the holder of the land trust. In such a case, it would not be unusual for the holder of the subordinated trust to assume the debt or pay out the lender, in order to protect against the loss of his interest in the ground. In the case where the second trust holder has a personal endorsement, he or she could seek a deficiency judgment against the individual who provided the endorsement; this assumes that the value of the property does not offer enough protection for the second trust holder, which is almost always the case. In cases where a purchase-money mortgage is to be subordinated and personally endorsed, the land seller will almost always require full financial disclosure of the individual providing the endorsement.

Although subordinated purchase-money mortgages can be used by large, relatively secure building companies to purchase prime ground at reasonable prices, they are most often available when the ground is priced at the high end of the market or it is in a marginal market area and poses a greater risk. In most land deals where a subordinated purchase-money mortgage can be negotiated, the purchase price is high and the seller will require an attractive interest rate. It is always easier to negotiate this type of financing in a buyer's market; sometimes under very favorable terms for those companies that provide comfort for the seller based on reputation and experience. From a builder's point of view, the subordinated purchase-money trust is the most desirable form of financing because it has the effect of reducing the up-front cash required to close a deal as well as reducing the owner's equity required by the lender.

USING LETTERS OF CREDIT

Letters of credit are third-party obligations, based on the financial standing of a company. Home builders sometimes use letters of credit to secure the performance of specific obligations. Such instruments might be used to:

◆ Provide a deposit under a land contract to secure the purchaser's obligations under the agreement.

◆ To secure a permit obligation, such as the construction of a driveway, storm drainage system, or street paving.

◆ To secure the performance of a custom builder with respect to a specific construction contract.

An *irrevocable letter of credit* is an absolute promise to pay in the event that certain conditions are not met. Such letters are typically issued by a commercial or savings bank, based upon a company's credit and ability to complete the work or meet the obligation. Letters of credit conserve cash, but they are typically written by the issuer for a fee of 1 to 2 percent of the face amount.

CHAPTER SUMMARY

Historically, commercial banks and thrifts have provided most of the financing required for the homebuilding industry.

Banks and thrifts are limited in the amount of funds that they can lend to one borrower, they are limited by maximum loan to value ratios, they must meet risk-based capital requirements, and they themselves can limit the amount of funds that they are willing to advance on a draw schedule.

The total loans to one borrower may not exceed 15 percent of the institutions unimpaired capital.

There are guidelines for banks and thrifts that restrict the amount of funds that they can advance for specific purposes. These restrictions are known as loans-to-value ratios and they are as follows:

1. Loans or advances on raw ground are limited to 65 percent of the appraised value.
2. Land development loans or land and advances are limited to 75 percent of the improved lot value.
3. Construction loans or finished land and advances on single-family (1 to 4 family residential construction) housing are limited to 85 percent of the appraised value at completion.

Participation loans are loans in which two or more lenders have agreed to fund a loan based on percentages of participation. The originating lender will generally service the loan for the participants.

A revolver is a provision in an ADC loan that allows the borrower to draw the construction funds down, pay them back, and then draw them down again.

An interest reserve is a requirement by a lender that establishes an escrow account from which interest payments can be made, thereby insuring the lender against a short-term default resulting from a failure to keep interest payments current.

A construction line of credit is a loan that permits the borrower to draw funds, up to a certain limit, as work progresses, pay the loan down as cash-flow permits, and then to draw the funds again over a specified period of time. Such lines of credit are negotiated with large institutional lenders, or a pool of lenders, and are typically secured by the assets of the company based on a security agreement.

An application for a construction loan should be a very formal and professional presentation, containing a detailed loan proposal prepared by the builder that, as a minimum, includes the following:

- A cover letter
- An area map locating the site
- A locator map showing the site and adjacent
- A number of pictures of the site
- A copy of the land contract
- A complete market study
- A project and cash budget
- A financing summary
- A summary of background
- Copies of relevant engineering and architectural plans

Construction loan underwriting is based on an appraisal of the property, the company's ability to complete the project based on historical performance, its demonstration of financial responsibility, its financial ability to carry the project in the event of an unforeseen problem, and the financial strength of the guarantors.

Appraisals are unbiased estimates of the nature, quality, value, or utility of an interest in specific real estate; they can be either an evaluation or a valuation. Appraisals are used to establish the current fair-market value of real estate and they are part of the underwriting process.

Contingent liability is a classification of obligations that are created by an owner as he or she endorses leases, guarantees loans or lines of credit, and guarantees performance by endorsing performance and payment bonds, as well as warranty agreements.

A loan commitment outlines the basic business provisions of the loan; it is typically, a summary letter of the business points that will be covered in detail in the legal documents that will follow. The building and loan agreement is a formal legal document and it is critical because it sets forth the terms and conditions of the loan.

A purchase money mortgage is a condition of sale requiring the seller to take back a note in lieu of cash for a portion of the land purchase price. A subordinated purchase-money mortgage is seller take-back financing that is in a second trust position to a bona fide acquisition, development, and/or construction loan.

PART III: CASH MANAGEMENT

6 MANAGING CASH AND REDUCING RISKS   73

7 FINANCIAL CONTROLS AND INSOLVENCY   99

CHAPTER 6

MANAGING CASH AND REDUCING RISKS

Effective cash management and the protection of assets can only result from well-directed effort. Understanding the forces that affect cash flow and the methods of reducing risks is a prerequisite for effective financial management. Cash flow can be significantly altered through the implementation of programs and activities designed to improve income, reduce costs and cost overruns, and conserving the cash that is generated through operations as well as from either debt or equity sources. Reducing risks and protecting both company and personal assets has more to do with policy, processes, and business practice than anything else. It is slightly more complicated, because it requires a broad understanding of both homebuilding and business management.

MAXIMIZING CASH FLOW

Cash flow arising from the normal operations of a business, is the difference between sales revenue and cash expenses including taxes. Other sources cash flows arise from the issuance of stock, borrowing, or from the sale of assets. Builders must understand the phenomenon of cash flow and understand how to improve it.

IMPROVING INCOME AND CASH FLOW DIVERSIFICATION

Home builders can diversify their product and services to include additional profit centers, such as major renovations, custom homes, or other income profit centers in order to improve income without substantially increasing general and administrative costs.

Pricing
Pricing will be discussed in depth in the next chapter, but it must be recognized as a primary activity effecting income or loss. Proper pricing must be established based on a very thoughtful process and senior management should monitor it carefully. While

pricing should be established in concert with the marketing staff, the marketing staff should not drive it. Too often, commissioned sales staff will resist price increases, even when they are entirely appropriate. The owner or president of a company should control pricing and increases should be the result of careful consideration following a discussion with both marketing and production personnel. Both sales volume and perceived value in the marketplace will become the forces that drive pricing decisions.

Cycle-Time and Inventory Turn

Nothing will do more to record income, produce cash, reduce costs, and increase margin than improving the build-time on new homes. By increasing inventory turn (turnover), the builder not only accelerates income, improves efficiency, and keeps his customers happy, but he also lowers *his* cost of money. Borrowed funds (both debt and equity) are paid back quicker resulting in lower interest charges.

Standard and Non-Standard Options

Both the process and the pricing policy are critical in the creation of income from standard and non-standard or special options. Standard options should be established with pricing at the time the product is developed. The pricing should be competitive, but insure a reasonable margin. The option strategy and pricing must be accepted by the sales personnel and presented to the buyer without negotiation. A purchasing manager should price non-standard options that are not declined, based on standard percentages that have been established by the company. The sales manager must then present this pricing without adverse comment. Most home builders are willing to make non-standard options available to accommodate the market, but they must be well paid for their effort; many home builders in competitive markets will price non-standard options with an 80 to 100 percent markup.

Production home builders must also keep in mind that some non-standard option requests should be declined. In cases where such requests will cause considerable disruption to the sales and production processes, they must be refused. In truth, the strength of the market will typically determine whether such non-standard option requests will be accepted or rejected, but in the event that they are accepted, the real cost of execution must be recognized.

Land Development

Although land development requires significantly more capital and additional risks for the home builder, it can generally help improve profit margins when it is handled properly. This is a natural activity for home builders because they have the ability to build and sell out a project at reduced prices in the event of a recession. Holding land during periods of recession can be extremely costly for land developers; most would rather build out in order to minimize losses. During such periods, there is typically no market for the finished lots and the limited new home market is motivated more by price; a market many builders refer to as "bottom feeders."

Final Payments and Escrows

Collecting final payments on custom contracts and escrows related closings must be a priority. Final payments on contracts must also be pursued earnestly and, where necessary, the legal remedies provided for in the contract must be employed sooner rather than later. The key to legal action will be the builder's level of competency. In most cases, where the home builder employs a quality building process combines with pro-active customer care, nothing will be lost as a result of the enforcement of legal rights. A customer who is unfair and unreasonable must be challenged if they attempt to withhold final payment without cause. In the event that a customer has cause, the builder must resolve the issues immediately in order to improve cash flow, preserve goodwill, and avoid the unnecessary risks related to non-performance.

Most home builders will not escrow funds at closing because such escrows can become difficult to collect; all too often, a homeowner will attempt to withhold such funds based on unreasonable demands. In most instances, a letter of acknowledgement with a reasonable assurance of completion is satisfactory and can be used successfully. In such cases, the builder's responsibility to complete the work and to satisfy the homeowner should be a very high priority. This will help other purchasers understand the value of such commitments. Home builders should keep in mind that some reasonable release provision must be established either by letter or a formal escrow agreement in those cases where closing escrows are unavoidable. Such a provision should *not* require the action of a homeowner to release funds.

Discounts
Discounts should be taken wherever they are offered. A 2 percent discount for payment by the 10th of each month will earn 37 percent when it is compounded annually. Keep in mind that a good buyer will negotiate the discount after he or she has negotiated the pricing; this is an important part of every contract negotiation and is often overlooked by inexperienced purchasing managers.

Advertising Credits and Model Home Rebates
A number of the major material manufacturers offer advertising credits and model home rebates. Find out which material manufacturers offer advertising credits and model home rebates. Try to take advantage of these opportunities wherever they exist and be sure to provide a method for tracking and collecting such credits and rebates.

Option Incentives
When it is necessary, use option incentives in lieu of price reductions in order to stimulate sales; the net effect on income will be lower. Lowering prices will always have a negative effect on perceived value in the minds of recent buyers and it has a tendency to build resentment. Using option incentives will generally protect the interests of earlier purchasers and protect against a potential devaluation of assets (where lot inventory exists). Where option incentives are used, they should be established and advertised for a specific period of time in order to create a sense of urgency; in the event that sales remain soft, option incentives can be extended.

Productivity
Increasing productivity will improve the bottom line. The keys to productivity are effective planning, well-defined processes and systems, written policy, a friendly supportive culture, and incentives based on performance.

REDUCING COSTS AND COST OVERRUNS

Every well-managed company should establish cost reduction initiatives designed to attack those areas of costs where history indicates a less than desirable performance. Such initiatives should be ongoing. After the company has improved in specific areas of concentrated effort, new areas should be established.

Earth Balance

Use more than one engineer to estimate earth balance on large projects. This will help insure against unnecessary and extraordinary cost overruns. Earth balance is a critical element of land development. Both importation and exportation of dirt can be a very costly activity; and such activity can damage finished streets and other site improvements when it occurs late in the process. Earth balance can also be a significant problem for a home builder buying finished lots for basement construction. Unless the temporary grades have been set to allow for a balanced basement excavation, the builder will face the costs related to the importation or exportation of dirt. This seems like a simple principle, but it has been a significant area of cost overruns for builders and land developers throughout the country.

Lumber Lists

Lumber lists that have resulted from a very careful product development process are hard to find. Such lists are critical to maintaining efficiency and reducing waste and theft. The list should be initially developed as a result of a material take-off, then the sticks should be counted in the field when the first production house or model is framed (a stick-count), and, finally, minor adjustments should be made as necessary following the first few production units. Once they are set, lumber lists should be locked down and any changes should require the signature of two or more responsible production employees. In large companies, any modification should require the signatures of the on-site construction manager, the area construction manager, the purchasing manager, and/or the VP of production. Unless these lists are controlled and protected, they will become the source of significant waste and theft.

Insurance

Insurance requirements should be established and submitted for bid at least every other year. Premiums vary and a policy of competitive bidding can produce considerable savings for even small companies. Builders, however, should keep in mind that in the event that their insurance company is unable to cover a claim, it does not release them from the responsibility. The question is how responsible is your insurance carrier? Often state funds can provide very competitive workman's compensation rates for the low-volume home builder or those who have suffered a recent "shock loss."

Partnership Program

A number of builders throughout the country are developing partnership programs with core trade contractors and suppliers. These informal relationships are largely based on "best prices" and pro-active support for the builder, with quick pay, a higher level of communication, and higher volume for the vendor. In many cases, the builder will host a luncheon twice a year and present a very carefully prepared production agenda with an emphasis on production flow, critical requirements for improvement, and a discussion of customer care performance.

Competitive Bidding

A competitive bidding process should be required for all core trades and material suppliers. Even in companies with a partnership program, a policy of competitive bidding will help insure "best prices." Bids should always be based on final plans, specifications, and scopes of work, and should be recorded for comparison upon receipt. Prior to final selection, bids should be reviewed and approved by two or more individuals including the on-site construction manager. In large companies, such decisions should be made by appropriate representatives of both construction and purchasing and should include field staff, a purchasing manager, and one or more senior managers. A formal bid process will insure competitive pricing and also provide the required back-up to support the decision in the event that the decision is ever questioned.; it will also insure that the motive for contracting is valid and in the best interest of the company.

Casual Labor

Poorly directed casual labor will result in errors, confusion, and low productivity. This is an area of abuse or neglect in many medium- and high-volume homebuilding organizations and it has the effect of increasing costs considerably. If casual labor is to be used, someone must be directly responsible for its management and oversight. In large companies, it is often more cost effective to employ punch-out technicians, service technicians, and general field labor rather than treating them as casual labor and employing them through temporary labor service companies. As employees, they can be held to a higher standard, expected to work in accordance with policy and job descriptions, and they are typically subject to more thoughtful management.

Solid Waste Disposal

Solid waste disposal is a costly item for home builders. Recycling should be enforced wherever possible. Demo boxes should be packed tight and restricted for construction use only. This can be accomplished in most cases by requiring trade contractors and employees to break cardboard boxes down, knock form material apart, and place waste rather than just throwing it in the box. It is then advisable for the on-site managers to use a backhoe (either as a favor or a requirement of the plumbing contractor) to compress the box whenever possible and to place a sign at the box that indicates that it is for construction waste only. Some home builders will require the drywall contractor to scrap units out and remove the waste from the construction site, although this does not always result in lower costs.

New homeowners can sometimes unnecessarily increase costs by using construction waste containers for household waste. It generally takes little effort to prevent new homeowners from using these dumpsters for household waste. A sign and some effort to locate violators will usually do the trick. If such abuse is ignored by the site-manager, it generally gets worse as more families move in.

Advertising

Advertising expense is typically a very significant component of marketing soft costs. Advertising is expensive and all too often it is overused in a seller's market. Advertising should reflect the need for sales on specific projects. Ads that have been planned must be pulled where sales are strong and little is to be gained by running the ad. Builders must remain flexible in terms of advertising commitments, and this is even more important in a seller's market. This requires coordination and focus on the part of the individual placing and managing the advertising campaigns.

While institutional advertising can be an effective way of building product recognition and reputation, most home builders should use it sparingly. Nothing will do more to enhance reputation than the word of mouth advertising that results from pro-active customer care. Generally speaking, builders of fewer than 100 homes per year should use institutional advertising sparingly and remain more flexible in terms of their advertising commitments.

Collateral Marketing Material

The collateral material used to market new homes can be very costly if it becomes necessary to reprint it in order to overcome changes resulting from a poor product development process. In cases where plans, specifications, and standard options are not well thought out, reprints and display adjustments become all too necessary. In order to overcome the contingent liability created by poorly coordinated marketing materials resulting in reprints and display corrections. Product development and marketing programs must be coordinated with a great deal of thought up front. Where this does not occur, it will have the effect of inflating marketing soft costs. Home builders must take the time to understand their markets and develop their product carefully in order to eliminate these unnecessary costs.

Provision for Poor Soils

Every direct cost budget should have some provision for the additional costs related to poor soils. This is not intended as a substitute for soils studies, but rather to handle the miscellaneous costs related to poor soils that were not anticipated as a result of a soils study. All too often, such costs appear as cost overruns merely because they have not been anticipated and provided for. Where such a provision exists, it should be monitored and adjusted based on experience.

Buying Cooperatives

Some low-volume home builders have found success through the formation of buying cooperatives. This is a group of small builders that create an alliance for the purpose of obtaining the better prices resulting from higher volume.

Watering Landscaping

The failure to keep new landscaping watered can lead to costly replacements. On-site responsibility for watering must be established and door tags (with a copy to the file) should be used to remind homeowners to water lawns and shrubs during dry weather. These actions will help reduce costs, as well as minimizing disputes with homeowners.

CONSERVING CASH

It is surprising how effective a well-focused home builder can be at conserving cash. Up front, it is always easier to make a decision to use cash if it is available, but the effective home builder will conserve cash with the knowledge that it may be the difference between success and failure down the road.

Loan-To-Value Ratios

In most cases, it is in the company's best interest to maintain standard and normal maximum loan-to-value ratios on all commercial loans as well as acquisition, development, and construction financing. This is not always easy, because bank policies are sometimes more restrictive; some lenders will establish lower loan-to-value ratios by policy. This is an important point to focus on when targeting a construction lender. Reasonable leverage ratios should be maintained and they should be reflected in the business plan.

Accelerated Releases and Interest Reserves

Wherever possible, avoid accelerated releases on purchase money trusts and construction loan. As conditions of construction financing, these provisions amount to a reduction in the available loan amount. Accelerated releases can have a devastating effect on cash flow because they are almost always substantial; often 5 to 10 percent of the purchase price of the ground. In general, it is usually better to refuse such provisions in order to protect the health of a building business.

Deposits and Progress Payments

Get substantial deposits on construction contracts, with the right to use the funds, and front loaded progress payments wherever possible. With this comes the responsibility to protect the purchaser's interest by handling such funds responsibly. Funds released for a specific project should only be used for that project. Co-mingling of funds can only result in embarrassment or a possible violation of a fiduciary responsibility that may have very serious legal consequences. Each project should stand on it's own. In the event that there is a cash shortfall on a project, it must be resolved with equity funds only.

Capital Spending

Using operating funds to over-fund the purchase of fixed assets or land can be a fatal mistake and any such expenditure should be made carefully based on the company's liquidity position. In most cases, it is wiser to invest surplus cash in either passbook savings or sweep accounts and short-term bonds. This will enable the company to maintain liquidity and provide reserves for future cash demands while developing some nominal yield on the money. Wherever possible, significant capital expenditures should be planned for two or more years in advance. The investment in equipment should never deplete working capital. Management must be sure that the company is capable of meeting both the investment requirements and long-term cash payments associated with the purchase of automobiles, trucks, and heavy equipment such as loaders, backhoes, fork lifts, and the like. Capital investment is often necessary in order to produce efficient and competitive management or operations. Finding the balance between necessary spending to maintain efficiency or a competitive position and thoughtless or unnecessary spending is not always easy.

Leasing
Consider leasing carefully before making any purchase decisions. In many instances, it will be smarter to lease than it will be to buy. Be sure to analyze large purchases carefully in terms of potential savings and the effect such purchases will have on cash flow overall.

Postponing Purchases
Postponing large purchases at the end of the month can often help improve cash flow. Rather than taking that lumber drop at the end of the month, you may be able to push it off until the next billing period by scheduling it for the first of the following month.

Early Starts
Avoid incurring early startup costs on new projects. Costs are generally estimated on a timeline and it is critical to both budgets and cash flow that that timetable be maintained as closely as possible. Incurring early start-up expenses will only incur greater costs and reduce the available working capital.

REDUCING RISKS

Risk management is a critical activity for home builders. The risk of property damage or personal injury related to construction and other activities is constant; product liability and general liability related to operations is ongoing; and, the likelihood of litigation related to human resource management, contract disputes, or homeowner satisfaction is very high for those who fail to manage their business properly. Homebuilding is a very complicated business and home builders must do everything in their power to minimize risks and protect the assets of the company. There are essentially three ways to manage risks:

◆ Hire the right people and protect them.

◆ Reduce exposure through the implementation of sound policy, procedures, and processes.

◆ Insure against those risks that are likely to threaten the success of the company.

STAFFING

Companies are about people first and policies, procedures, and processes second. A company that is poorly directed from the top has a higher probability of success with the right people in key positions, but it is not likely that a company with sound direction and the wrong people will ever find real success. Staff should be recruited carefully, based largely on knowledge, experience, and the ability to communicate effectively. People skills are critical to maintaining a suitable culture and protecting the interests of the team. Applicants should be screened carefully in order to validate their qualifications; at a minimum, the process should include telephone screening, a preliminary interview, an in-depth interview, a background check, and reference checks. The strongest applicants will be those who are recommended by others that you know and respect. Once the team has been assembled, standards of performance, compensation, and culture will be the glue that binds the individuals together.

CULTURE

Much has been written recently about the culture of companies. Culture can be defined by a company's value system, the personality of the company, the behavior that is handed down from one employee to another, unwritten law defining what is or is not done, and, the way things are done in their company. In truth, it is all of these things. The written statements and actions must be established by those managers at the very top of an organization must establish it. Some essential elements of a benchmark homebuilding culture include:

◆ Promoting honest and ethical behavior

◆ Maintaining a professional bearing throughout the company

◆ Maintaining a quality building program and demonstrate high standards of quality

◆ Maintaining a customer focus, with an emphasis on customer care and post-settlement service

◆ Providing an open, supportive work environment for each employee with real concern for personal development and quality of life

◆ Hiring and training employees who are professional, respectful, and courteous to one another at all times

◆ Compensating employees based on performance and contribution

◆ Providing written policies, procedures, and processes that will enable employees

◆ Maintaining a high level of efficiency and productivity

◆ Maintaining a safe workplace

◆ Paying bills promptly and discounting wherever possible

◆ Demonstrating respect and concern for those with whom the company does business

◆ Demonstrating concern for the communities within which the company builds

◆ Applying standards uniformly and fairly

◆ Resolving complaints and disputes based on what is fair and reasonable

Culture should be established carefully and each member of the team should be given an opportunity to help create or modify. By providing an open forum, employees are extended the right to influence culture and policy merely by bringing their recommendations to the table. Senior management should discuss such recommendations and they should either be accepted or returned to the employee with an explanation of why the recommendation was declined. In ideal situations, the employee will have the opportunity to bring his recommendation to the table, present it, and be part of the discussion concerning its merits.

PLANNING

Planning has been covered in detail in the first three chapters of this book. Nothing will reduce risks more than a well-conceived business plan that includes both strategies and financial plans that have been discussed carefully and validated by a group of professionals with considerable experience. A killer business plan is a prerequisite for success and it will do more to mould a team and protect the assets of the company than any other single activity. Successful companies understand this and often provide annual planning retreats in order to provide an environment that permits a singular focus and a continuous exchange of ideas among key personnel. The secret to such retreats is organization and an opportunity for the general staff to make recommendations by providing information to those attending these retreats in advance.

USING CONSULTANTS

Consultants are extremely good sources for current facts and information in specific areas of interest. Companies can maintain a current level of expertise in core areas by using consultants on a regular basis. For these purposes, the term consultant refers to a broad group of professionals that have the ability of providing the company with current information on specific subjects. Just as decisions should be made based on facts, using consultants will improve the quality of those decisions and reduce risks inherent in bad decisions.

Marketing consultants, management consultants, financial consultants, soils engineers, structural engineers, and attorneys are just some of the professionals that can provide support and direction on an ongoing basis. A marketing consultant should provide a detailed market study for each major project during its feasibility period and it is advisable to update information relative to the major market area every year in order to remain current. Management consultants can help validate and improve policy, procedures, and processes. Financial consultants can be particularly useful in the creation of long-term strategies and plans for significant growth or expansion as well as fine-tuning financial plans for large projects. Soils and structural engineers should help train production staff and both can provide significant support for new projects and products under development.

Using attorneys to consult up front can minimize risks related to legal liabilities. In most organizations, attorneys conduct settlements and help create specific legal documents, such as letters of intent, land contracts, sales contracts, employment agreements and the like, but they are often overlooked as consultants by the low- or medium-volume home builder. As a home builder moves from low-volume to high-volume, the role of the attorney often becomes a little more involved. Among other areas, attorneys should be used to review established human resource policy and suggest changes that will help reduce the risks related to human resource management. Due to current trends in labor litigation, it is particularly important for a labor law attorney to understand the human resource management policies and procedures adopted by the company.

> *The release of escrows and the completion of site improvements that are bonded are critical for land developers. The longer escrows and bonds are open, the greater the liability for damage. Experienced developers will find ways to complete their work and release their bonds and escrows quickly.*

LAND AND LAND DEVELOPMENT

Risks related to the purchase and development of land are significant and unless home builders understand the nature of these risks, they may put their companies in a higher risk position than is necessary. Some tips to reduce risks related to land and land development include the following:

Location

Location must be right, you can overcome a weak house built on a prime lot, but never a weak house built in a poor location. Projects that are impacted by super highways, high tension power lines, stone quarries, arsenic soils, proximity to solid waste landfills, and the like all pose higher risks and those risks must be recognized by land developers and home builders. Such environmentally sensitive land could easily be rejected by the market or perhaps require a significant devaluation as a result of new environmental impact debates.

Feasibility Studies

The quality of feasibility studies is critical in terms of reducing risks for the home builder. A well-focused feasibility study must be conducted that is based on a carefully developed process that includes a market study with a competitive analysis, a Phase I environmental impact study, and a soils study, as well as well-conceived strategies and financial plans that have taken alternatives into account.

Cost Estimates

Initial engineering and cost estimates are critical. Be sure that initial engineering is accurate, particularly with respect to topography. The most critical area of land development estimating is the calculation of cuts and fills and estimates for the importation or exportation of dirt. Avoid such risks by using two or more professional engineers for earthwork calculations; the benefits will generally far outweigh the additional costs.

Retaining Walls

Retaining walls can provide additional risks related to potential failures. As builders and developers attempt to work with more difficult land plans, they are often required to build retaining walls in a variety of soil conditions that are more complicated and subject to greater engineering requirements. Unless the design and construction process includes adequate engineering and certifications during construction, the resulting risks are considerably greater than they have to be. Structural engineers, with the benefit of a soils study, should design structural retaining walls, they should be inspected and certified during the construction and backfill operations, and, a structural engineer should certify them upon completion. The plans, specifications, reports, certifications, and any photographs taken during construction should then be retained in a file until the statute of limitations has expired. Structural retaining walls can fail long after they are constructed and in such cases, the focus will typically be on the quality of construction and the backfill operations.

Options on Ground

Option ground wherever possible in order to eliminate the long-term risks and substantial carrying-costs associated with land inventory.

A QUALITY BUILDING PROGRAM

A quality building program not only reduces callbacks and risks related to product liability and on-site safety, it also provides a higher level of confidence for both consumers and staff and it reduces unnecessary costs and delays related to corrections or repairs late in the production process. This is a primary consideration for the satisfaction of customers and a serious reduction in construction costs for both the home builder and vendors. Building a quality product and documenting it will also help fend off those who might otherwise criticize unfairly.

The ability to defend against disputes and disagreements resulting from the unfair and unreasonable demands of others is a re requirement of every home builder. This ability is a natural by-product of the organization described in this book. The policies, procedures, and processes set the ground-work for the level of communication and documentation that is necessary to reduce such risks.

A quality building program generally consists of seven major requirements:

◆ Well-qualified staff

◆ Uniform contracts, specifications and scopes of work

◆ Involvement of engineers

◆ Involvement of customers

◆ Required frame and floor checks

◆ Quality assurance program

◆ Oversight inspections

Well-Qualified Staff

Production staff must be well qualified. Some years ago, superintendents were used to manage residential construction sites. These employees were largely responsible for the oversight of the various trades working on the project. Today, the responsibilities of these on-site construction managers is much more complicated. They must not only provide the oversight for the trades, who are poorly trained in many cases, but they must also play a critical role in planning, purchasing, sales coordination, and customer care. These are complicated positions and require a much higher level of management expertise and communication skills. Any attempt to build houses or develop ground with staff that is not knowledgeable and experienced can only result in higher risks and disappointment.

Uniform Contracts, Specifications, and Scopes of Work

Developing uniform labor and material contracts, project specifications, and scopes of work will help everyone understand the terms and conditions of construction. These are basic documents that provide a clear understanding of the materials to be used and the responsibilities for construction. When combined with the architectural and engineering plans, they become the enabling documents for construction managers and trade contractors. They provide legal protections along with clear statements related to specific areas of the construction process.

These documents should be used for management purposes only, and should not be confused with the sales plans and feature sheets that are often used as exhibits and attached to the new home contracts of sale used with purchasers. As management tools, they will help employees understand both the product and the construction process. While plans and specifications are often given to purchasers of new custom homes, they should never be given to purchasers of production homes. Such materials have been developed with the product at considerable expense to the company and should be protected. They should only be provided to those who have the need and are part of the production process.

The Involvement of Engineers

On production projects, soils engineers should be used for all footing inspections and certifications should be placed in the permanent lot file located in the main office Structural engineers should also be employed during the product development process and to make field inspections where required. Reports resulting from such field inspections should also be placed in the permanent lot file in the main office. In the event that a truss repair becomes necessary, the certified repair detail should also be placed in the permanent file in the main office. Engineering documentation should be an important part of the lot history and the permanent file (either hard copies or scan files of the documents where electronic files are maintained) should reflect it. In the event that an issue arises after completion, the proper documentation will be available for those responding to the issue.

Customer Involvement

Every home builder should encourage customer involvement during the construction process. Such involvement should, however, be controlled and in accordance with company policy. In addition to site inspections that may be scheduled by the purchaser, each purchaser should meet with the construction manager or his representative on at least three occasions during the construction process:

◆ A *pre-construction meeting* should be scheduled with the project manager and the sales agent for the purpose of discussing the process and reviewing the proposed construction including both standard and non-standard options.

◆ A *pre-drywall walk* should be conducted by the construction manager prior to concealment for the purpose of reviewing the framing and rough-ins prior to drywall.

◆ A formal, disciplined, and almost scripted *orientation* should be conducted by the construction or service manager upon completion. The purpose of the orientation is to demonstrate the house, provide information and a discussion of post-settlement service procedures, and finally, to walk the house for the purpose of inspecting fit and finishes throughout.

Each inspection should include the execution of a single-page document that memorializes the meeting, the substance of the conversation, and any concerns expressed by the purchaser. In each case, a copy of the report, acknowledged by the purchaser, should be placed in the permanent lot file in order to confirm discussions and document the resolution of issues or questions.

Required Frame and Floor Checks

In order to insure a higher level of quality, on-site field construction managers should be required to conduct frame and floor checks. All framing should be checked carefully prior to concealment and all floor sheathing should be checked carefully prior to the application of floor finishes. Using a high-visibility paint and a keel, framing and floor sheathing should be marked in areas where adjustments are required. Requiring formal frame and floor checks will help reduce minor defects, such as bowed walls and floor squeaks that could become costly repairs after completion.

A Quality Assurance Program

An effective quality assurance program for home builders consists of a detailed checklist covering every reasonable concern related to framing and rough-in stage of construction. A typical list might consist of 80 to 100 items set in trade categories that include framing (including windows, exterior doors, and stairs), party-wall construction (where appropriate), HVAC rough, plumbing rough, electrical rough, air stopping, and insulation. This checklist should be reviewed and signed off by the on-site construction manager with a copy to the permanent lot file in the main office. In the event of deficiencies, they should be noted with corrective action. Although most experienced construction managers resist such lists, they can significantly improve the quality of construction, minimize mistakes, reduce costs, and provide evidence of a higher building standard.

Oversight Inspections

Oversight is critical for quality in construction. On-site construction managers must walk their houses every day and area construction supervisors must validate both the process and the standards of quality. The work of tradesmen must be inspected for both quality and to insure safe working conditions; materials must be inspected to insure that they meet reasonable standards of quality; and structural elements must be inspected for performance. Oversight inspections will not only improve construction quality, protect against waste, and help maintain a safe workplace, but they will also inspire a higher level of confidence in homebuyers.

Some builders have gone as far as requiring the painting contractor to vacuum out the house prior to prepping for paint and applying a prime coat on the interior. In well-managed building companies, most quality issues after completion center around fit and finish. Attempts to improve fit and finish should focus on the scopes of work; by inserting key language in scopes for the core finish trades, a significant improvement can be made.

A quality-building program will help the home builder do it right the first time and void costly disputes and unnecessary adjustments to finished work after completion. Product quality is often an indicator of a company's ability to compete and the effectiveness of its management practice. A formal process with well-documented effort will not only improve quality and reduce costs, but it will also reduce the risks of disputes and litigation in an area of operations where defending against unreasonable complaints can be very difficult.

SAFETY IN THE WORKPLACE

Maintaining safety in the workplace is an absolute requirement in order to reduce the risk of property loss, personal injury, or death. An effective safety program will protect assets, provide security, and generally reduce the risks related to construction activity or an office environment; it can help reduce the potential number and severity of accidents, avoid litigation related to safety violations, reduce workers' compensation premiums, minimize the possibility of fines, and insure compliance with the law. The preparation of a safety program must be based on specific requirements or considerations, which include the following:

◆ Federal, state, and local regulations

◆ The nature of company operations

◆ Insurance company requirements

◆ The legal impact or the potential liability that such a program may create for the company

CUSTOMER CARE AND POST-SETTLEMENT SERVICE

Providing customer care is the responsibility of every employee including the president of the company. Unless every employee is committed to maintaining a customer focus and helping customers wherever they can, the company will never achieve the highest level of customer satisfaction and referral sales. While each employee has his specific responsibilities in the homebuilding organization, each must be willing to talk to customers and help wherever they can. Throughout the process, the on-site sales manager or sales agent must act as an advocate for the homebuyer and shepherd them through the process; supervisors in every area must be willing to get involved with the customer in order to provide information or resolve an issue; and, the president or a designated vice president should be prepared to accept the ultimate responsibility to manage those who are unfair and unreasonable.

Post-Settlement service is best provided by a separate department and should not be provided by on-site construction managers accept in very small companies where the costs of a departmentalized service department are prohibitive. There are several basic advantages of a centralized warranty service:

◆ It gives the company more control over the quality of service.

◆ It allows the on-site construction manager to concentrate on the construction process and avoid the time-consuming tasks of service management.

◆ It produces a higher level of confidence on the part of homeowners. Nothing will do more to reduce homeowner liability and the loss of goodwill than these simple, but important policy provisions related to customer care and post-settlement service.

INSURANCE

The risks related to home building can be reduced through insurance and an effective risk management program will include adequate coverage based on the size and scope of the operation. Typically, home builders will carry the following types of insurance coverage:

General Liability
This is required coverage that protects the company against losses resulting from operations. Liability insurance is sometimes referred to as defense coverage because it serves no purpose other that to protect the building company from claims brought against it by third parties.

Property Damage
Property damage insurance consists of two types: (1) damage to work in process, and (2) damage to company-owned property. Most property damage policies for home builders have an XCU exclusion, which excludes coverage for explosion, collapse, and underground damage. Often builders rely on subcontractors for this coverage, but, in that event, it must be confirmed at the time of contracting any blasting, excavating, or trenching.

Employee Coverage
This includes all of the forms of insurance for employees. Typically it includes workers' compensation, social security, unemployment, and disability insurance.

Auto Coverage

This coverage is designed to protect the company from liability and property damage claims arising out of accidents involving company owned vehicles, and may include comprehensive coverage for fire, theft, and collision for non-owned and hired vehicles.

An Umbrella Policy

A commercial umbrella liability policy is a relatively inexpensive way to provide additional coverage against a catastrophic third-party claim. Due to the risks related to homebuilding and the very high awards, which now occur in bodily-injury cases, this form of increased coverage is advisable.

Title Insurance

Title insurance protects an owner or mortgage from any loss due to defects in the title to the property due to liens or encumbrances, except for those liens and encumbrances stated in the policy as existing at the time that the policy is issued. Mortgagee's title insurance is typically required by lenders and is generally paid for by the builder as a cost of settlement.

Insurance expense represents a substantial operating cost for home builders and it is a major consideration. After determining the limits of insurance required for the company, those annual needs should be shopped carefully in order to guarantee that the company obtains the broadest coverage at the most competitive rates. As indicated above, this can best be accomplished through competitive bidding initiated by the company.

It is important that the insurer be financially responsible in order to meet the requirements covered in the policy and that should be a primary qualification for any bidder. After financial capacity has been established, pricing should be the driving factor. That is not to say that the service typically provided by the agent is of little consequence. It is important, but the client should demand reasonable service that includes a semi-annual review of operations and insurance coverage in force, and an annual evaluation of year-end performance and requirements contemplated for the upcoming year.

In order to be safe, building companies should *not* underestimate annual payroll and gross revenue, which are used to establish premiums for worker's compensation and general liability insurance. This would create a substantial cash demand at the time of an insurance audit. The final premium for this insurance is based on actual payroll and revenues at the end of the policy period. It is always wise to predict these key targets accurately or to adjust them periodically in order to avoid a substantial assessment at the end of the policy period.

TAX OBLIGATIONS

Local, state, and federal payroll taxes, real property taxes, and estimated income taxes must be deposited or paid on time in order to meet financial obligations and maintain a more conservative and predictable cash position. In most cases, avoiding the estimated payment of income taxes will only produce a larger demand for cash at the end of the year. By making provisions for the payment of income taxes throughout the year, the company avoids the risks associated with "checkbook management," which is the tendency to spend or invest accumulated cash without recognizing the substantial obligation that will produce a future need for cash.

Payroll tax deposits are both a moral and legal obligation of the company and any attempt to manipulate them can only lead to embarrassment or worse. In most cases where such deposits are not made in order to meet some other cash requirement, every other method of leverage has been exhausted and the company has reached a position of insolvency. Such actions can only make a bad situation worse; the reality is that the company must either be liquidated or restructured for new equity funding.

BENCHMARK COMPANIES AND ADVISORY BOARDS

Business owners and senior managers are charged with the responsibility of setting direction and establishing the policies, practices, and processes that are required to keep companies healthy. In order to do this effectively, they require a great deal of knowledge and experience. Following the lead of benchmark companies and creating an advisory board can be very effective methods of reducing risks and increasing the quality of decisions by creating a broader knowledge base. Successful professionals know where to find help and when to reach out for it.

Home builders should identify those companies in their markets that have a track record of success, the respect of the industry, and an exceptional professional standing in the community. They can learn from these benchmark companies simply by understanding what works for them and then emulating it. It is also advisable to find other benchmark homebuilding companies that are similar in size in non-competing markets, that will share financial and management information for the common purpose of improvement. Such an open exchange of ideas, financial information, and management practices can only improve the quality of a business and the ability of its directors to make sound decisions. It also has the effect of creating a much broader network and sphere of influence, which can only be healthy for the future of a homebuilding company.

If they are developed carefully, advisory boards can provide a great deal of support for business organizations. In many cases, such boards are informal in nature in new companies and become more formal as the company grows and develops. The key to an effective board is the knowledge and experience of its members. Advisory board members should be made up of owners, investors with a business background and professionals with substantial knowledge and experience. In order to be effective, such board members must be able to provide significant support in critical areas and they must be paid, compensation has the effect of insuring a higher level of focus, organization, and performance. Today, building successful companies is more about team building than it is the success of a single entrepreneur; markets are complicated and the level of competition is fierce in most cases.

PAYMENT POLICY

Maintaining a policy of current pay and taking discounts will not only improve the quality of trade partnerships, help insure "best prices," and improve the bottom line, it will also help maintain the integrity of the business plan and provide a safety net in the event of a temporarily tight cash position. The business plan should reflect a current pay policy, and operating within that plan is a requirement of success. In the event that cash becomes tight for any reason, the company has the opportunity of extending payment terms to thirty or forty-five days without creating considerable concern on the part of employees and vendors.

In the event that payment terms are extended beyond thirty days, a representative of the company should discuss such a condition with vendors and staff in advance. Keeping everyone informed demonstrates that the company recognizes its financial responsibilities to its vendors and it also extends an opportunity for its vendors to express concern in the event that they may also be facing a tight cash position; usually such situations can be resolved easily if the conversations occur in advance.

WORKING CAPITAL AND LEVERAGE

Working capital is the difference between current assets and current liabilities.

$$\text{Working Capital} = \text{Current Assets} - \text{Current Liabilities}$$

Maintaining adequate working capital is probably a fundamental of minimizing risks and reducing the stress of owning a homebuilding company. In addition, it is a requirement for growth and development and it should be a focus of owners, presidents, financial managers, and controllers. Adequate working capital is generally reflected in business plans and any change should be the result of a condition that was not anticipated in the plan. Inadequate working capital can create a serious hardship for home builders and their staff; success in competitive markets depends on the ability to pay vendors promptly and meeting other financial commitments. Builders that find themselves with inadequate working capital often make the decision to become "slow pay," which is using their credit with trade contractors and suppliers to overcome the problem. Unfortunately, this is not always a temporary condition and it has the potential to destroy the reputation of an otherwise good builder. It also puts the company in a position of higher risk. If the condition is not corrected quickly the company will lose credibility and create considerable concern in the minds of employees and those that do business with it.

In most cases, home builders become over-leveraged as a result of on-going losses that erode equity. The condition develops after startup and it can destroy the company's ability to secure financing. The only cure is to obtain additional equity capital or to become profitable quickly. Builders that face this condition should accept the reality of the situation and begin developing a business plan that will improve the condition and provide the potential income necessary to attract additional equity investors. Leverage must be limited to normal levels and it is critical that both the business plan and the performance of the company reflect it.

CONDOMINIUM ASSOCIATIONS

Condominium associations pose additional risks for builders and developers. Historically, condominium associations have, on occasion, become a vehicle for disgruntled homeowners to gain support for class action litigation with little personal financial exposure. Companies that build condominiums must recognize the additional risks up front and limit such liability wherever possible. In addition to limiting liability as outlined in the policies, procedures, and processes discussed earlier, the builder can create a separate entity for such projects, maintain a closer relationship with homeowners, develop favorable relationships with association officers and board members, and maintain a highly visible and active role in the association. Those with well-established reputations for customer satisfaction should probably build condominiums. For those who build these projects without such experience and reputation, the risks are much greater.

BUILD THE COMPANY FOR SALE

As building companies mature, they often become acquired or go public themselves. This affords an opportunity for the owner or owners of a successful company to eliminate contingent personal liabilities, to cash out, or, perhaps, to leverage the success of a small- or medium-volume business. The companies that are most successful often go on to acquire other building companies in order to accelerate growth and development and to take advantage of economies of scale. Historically, most acquiring companies have been either large, well-established public companies or new roll-up companies that purchase and merge a number of smaller building companies in geographically diverse markets, in order to go public. Today, there are a number of very large, successful companies that have remained privately held and have the potential to expand their markets through acquisitions. Many of these companies have chosen to avoid the pressure of ever increasing demands for improved financial performance created by a large group of public stockholders. Because they are privately held, these companies can represent unique opportunities for acquisitions; they tend to offer a little more flexibility for the owners of the acquired companies.

New home building companies should be developed for a potential sale in the future. Critical requirements for the sale of a company include the development of well-conceived business plans, written policies, standardized procedures, the development of effective processes, a high level of customer satisfaction, a reputation for effective management, and a substantial earnings history. These are the same requirements for a successful homebuilding company. Whether the company is ever sold is immaterial, it will always remain an option for the owner or owners. Building a company for sale can only have the effect of reducing risks, improving the quality of management, establishing a benchmark position in the market, and creating a sense of anticipation on the part of owners and management staff.

JOINT VENTURES, LIMITED PARTNERSHIPS, AND LIMITED LIABILITY COMPANIES

Home builders use joint ventures, limited partnerships, and limited liability companies in order to take advantage of opportunities extended by investors that want to participate in specific projects or perhaps, to improve the return on company investment. Such organizations will help limit liability on the part of the owners and investor, provide for separate accounting records for a specific project or group of projects, and organize responsibilities for the participants.

Once the organization has been capitalized and established as a going concern, new projects will generally be undertaken as separate entities controlled by the parent company. Many builders establish joint venture entities, limited partnerships, or limited liability companies to isolate specific projects from other company activity. Such individual projects are then financed as separate entities with the guarantee of repayment by the parent company and its owners. While significant operating liability may be reduced and accounting is cleaner where separate entities are used for each new project or group of projects, the financial liability created by the ADC loans may be reduced, but never eliminated. By introducing a joint venture partner or substantial equity capital on such loans provided by limited partners or limited liability investors, a building company can effectively reduce its own financial exposure.

Home builders are well advised to consider joint ventures, limited partnerships, and limited liability companies carefully. They all produce substantial fiduciary responsibilities and require additional administrative effort. Where they are successful and investors experience substantial returns on their investment, they can be very effective and even establish an investment pool for the builder; but litigation can be a natural by-product of such entities where performance falls well below that which has been represented.

Joint Venture

An entity typically formed by two or more individuals, companies, or a mix of both individuals and companies acting in concert to complete a specific project or group of projects. These entities are typically established to limit liability by spreading the risks. The terms and conditions typically provide for the builder to receive a fixed fee per unit that is designed to reimburse out-of-pocket administrative and indirect costs, for the investors to receive a fixed return on their invested capital with a "kicker" or fixed share of projected profits, and the builder generally takes whatever is left when the project is complete.

Limited Partnership

Limited partnerships have become an excellent vehicle for privately owned building companies to raise equity capital. Such entities are generally based on a very formal document known as an *offering memorandum* which typically includes information related to the investment proposal and the terms and conditions of the investment, as well as a subscription agreement and a detailed investors questionnaire. In most cases, qualified investors must meet the following criteria:

◆ Investment is often limited to a $100 thousand minimum unit.

◆ Investors must be experienced with a substantial net worth; known as a sophisticated investor.

◆ Investors must be more than 21 years of age.

◆ Units must be purchased for the investor's own account.

◆ The investor must demonstrate the financial ability to bear the economic risk of the entire investment.

◆ The speculative nature of the investment must be acknowledged.

◆ The investor must demonstrate adequate liquidity to cover current needs and personal contingencies.

The Limited Liability Company

Most states have enacted legislation recognizing the LLC as an acceptable business entity. In fact, many new homebuilding entities are being created with a limited liability company as the parent company. An LLC protects investors in real estate transactions by limiting liability while providing the flow-through taxation available in partnerships (which are not recommended as a viable entity for home builders) and S corporations. In some cases, one of its members may assume personal liability for all of the entity's debts; in such a case, that member must own at least 1 percent of the LLC and have a net worth of at least 10 percent of the total contributions of the LLC, or substantial assets that creditors can reach. To qualify as a LLC, it must not have two of the following corporate characteristics:

◆ Limited liability

◆ Free transferability of ownership

◆ Continuity of life

◆ Centralized management

Many LLCs have been able to qualify for their status by:

◆ Limiting free transferability by requiring that each member be prohibited from transferring their interest to a non-member without the consent of a majority of the other members.

◆ Providing a lack of continuity of life by providing for a dissolution of the LLC upon the death, insanity, bankruptcy, retirement, resignation or expulsion of any member.

◆ Denying centralized management by providing a statement in the operating agreement that states that the LLC is managed by the members exclusively in their capacity as members; if the owners designate one or more of its members as managers, the IRS may still rule favorably if the member manager owns at least 20 percent of the LLC.

PROTECTING PERSONAL ASSETS

Protecting personal assets, is the most critical rule of personal financial planning and it becomes more important to home builders and land developers because substantial contingent liabilities are created by personal endorsements and/or guarantees. Some simple methods of protecting personal assets for home builders and their senior staff include:

◆ Forming a corporation of limited liability company

◆ Denying or limiting personal endorsements and guarantees

◆ Establishing irrevocable and living trusts

◆ Liquidating, selling, or reorganizing

◆ Going public

Form a Corporation or Limited Liability Company

Forming a corporation can help limit personal liability, but there are some requirements that must be acknowledged in order to reduce the potential for additional personal liability. Directors and officers of corporations have a duty of obedience and must act within their authority. In some jurisdictions, an officer or director who exceeds his authority may be held personally liable to the corporation for unauthorized acts, and in other jurisdictions, may be liable if he or she intentionally or negligently exceeds his authority. While this principle of law may seem remote to the small home builder operating as a corporation, it has much more significance for the directors and officers of medium- and large-volume corporations.

In cases where the outstanding shares are held by a small number of individuals, who are often family, relatives, and friends who are active in the business (referred to as a closely held corporation), it is advisable to maintain normal corporate formalities. Holding required meetings of the board of directors and shareholders, and maintaining copies of the minutes of those meetings is important; maintaining required minutes and other records that demonstrate that the corporation is not merely a front for an individual attempting to limit liability and to use the corporation merely to deny a plaintiff due process of law. A failure to provide an adequate financial basis or a failure to conduct business in accordance with the articles of incorporation and by-laws could result in the ability of a litigant to pierce the corporate veil and establish personal liability. It is also important to note that the directors of a corporation not only have a fiduciary responsibility to maximize the value of the company, but they also have an economic responsibility to:

◆ Review and approve both strategic and financial plans

◆ Select senior management, evaluate its performance, and establish its compensation

◆ Monitor the financial results of the company

◆ Ensure the integrity of financial data and the existence of adequate record keeping and control systems through verification by an independent auditor

As discussed above, limited liability companies will also offer significant protection of the personal assets of home builders. Unfortunately, the contingent liabilities created by personal endorsements and guarantees are, for the most part, inescapable for home builders.

In those cases where a proposal is attractive in terms of both risk and return, the financial character of the borrower or borrowers often becomes the focus of the lender and the desire to make such a loan may be based largely on that financial character. That is to say, that a private or institutional investor will carefully evaluate the attributes or qualities of a borrower based largely on reputation, credit rating, professional standing, and the quality of the loan request. It is the strength of this financial character that will sometimes permit a lender to compromise when negotiating personal guarantees with the officers of such companies.

Deny or Limit Personal Endorsements and Guarantees

It is the obligation of lenders to try to control or limit their risks in business transactions. In order to preserve capital, they must evaluate the potential of the transaction, the inherent risks associated with it, and its relative status in terms of other loan opportunities. In every case, they will attempt to secure their loans with collateral and obtain personal guarantees in order to reduce risks. Such efforts will generally create contingent liabilities for borrowers in the form of loan guarantees or restrictions on personal assets that have been pledged to secure such business loans.

In order to limit such contingent liability, borrowers must negotiate their financial exposure with lenders before the terms of the loan are finalized. After a loan is finalized, it is next to impossible for a borrower to secure a release of liability before the loan has been paid off. Borrowers must make every reasonable effort to obtain non-recourse loans wherever possible and to limit personal liability wherever they can. In order to accomplish this, borrowers must be realistic about the strength of their loan proposals, the company's ability to repay such loans, and its financial character.

Wherever possible, borrowers should use *capped* or *partial guarantees* by limiting personal losses to a specific sum of money. Often, personal guarantees can be limited to the amount of a loan, which is not protected by collateral. In addition to capped guarantees, builders will often limit liability by:

◆ Guaranteeing collection rather than repayment of the debt; in the case of a default, the lender must proceed against the collateral first and only then can they proceed against personal assets and then only for the balance due.

◆ Withholding the endorsement of a spouse which would protect personal assets held jointly or solely in his name.

◆ Excluding selected personal assets from the guarantee such as a residence, certain securities, or, perhaps, proceeds from a trust.

◆ By requiring other individuals to share in the endorsement, the endorsement should be limited to a specific share of the potential debt.

◆ Establishing a time limit on the endorsement; the guarantee would expire on a certain date as long as all of the terms and conditions of the loan have been met.

◆ The lender should be required to go after business assets before personal assets.

Irrevocable and Living Trusts

Establishing both irrevocable and living trusts can be effective ways to protect and control assets. Irrevocable trusts can be established with children or a spouse as beneficiaries to hold assets, and a living trust can be created for relatives and/or charitable organizations in order to protect some personal income. This form of liability protection is usually used with family trusts for sons and daughters. Under current law, after tax contributions can be made to such individual living trusts in the amount of $10,000 per year ($20,000 in the case of contributions from both husband and wife) without tax consequences to the trust. Interest and dividend income from such trusts is generally distributed annually to the beneficiaries with tax consequences. The principle of the trust is generally distributed, based on an age schedule established by the trust documents, without tax consequences to the individual or organization.

Liquidate, Sell, or Reorganize

Builders may consider the possibility of liquidating or selling the company in order to escape personal liability. This is particularly true of those builders facing retirement. Another possibility is for the builder to reorganize the company and remove himself or herself as an endorser or guarantor. In such cases, one or more substitute endorsers or guarantors, usually senior officers who are provided for in a plan of succession, replace the original builder on all endorsements and guarantees.

Going public

As mentioned earlier, some builders will go public in order to release personal endorsements on all borrowing and other contingent liabilities. They may go public through a new initial offering, or by merging with or becoming acquired by an existing public company. These are all acceptable methods of releasing personal liability for a building company. Many medium- and large-volume home builders have gone public in order to release personal liability, as well as to provide for the succession of the business.

Personal holding companies or corporations, established to control personal assets such as real estate, automobiles, investments, company stock, bank accounts and the like, by placing them under the corporate control of others, seldom work for home builders. Most construction loans are approved based on the personal guarantee and personal net worth of the borrower or borrowers.

CHAPTER SUMMARY

Effective cash management and the protection of assets can only result from well-directed effort. Understanding the forces that affect cash flow and the methods of reducing risks is a prerequisite for effective financial management.

Reducing risks and protecting both company and personal assets has more to do with policy, processes, and business practice than anything else.

Operating cash flow arise from the normal operations of a business, which is, in essence, the difference between sales revenue and cash expenses including taxes; other cash flows arise from the issuance of stock, borrowing, or from the sale of assets.

Each project should stand on it's own; in the event that there is a cash shortfall on a project, it must be resolved with equity funds only.

There are essentially three ways to manage risks: 1) hire the right people and protect them, 2) reduce exposure through the implementation of sound policy, procedures, and processes; and 3) insure against those risks that are likely to threaten the success of the company.

Companies are about people first and policies, procedures, and processes second. Once the team has been assembled, standards of performance, compensation, and culture will be the glue that binds the individuals together.

It is tangible and real, and the written statements and actions of those managers at the very top of an organization must establish it.

Nothing will reduce risks more than a well-conceived business plan that includes both strategies and financial plans that have been discussed carefully and validated by a group of professionals with considerable experience.

Decisions should be made based on facts; using consultants will improve the quality of those decisions and reduce risks inherent in bad decisions.

Risks related to the purchase and development of land are significant and unless home builders understand the nature of these risks, they may put their companies in a higher risk position than is necessary.

A quality building program not only reduces callbacks and risks related to product liability and on-site safety, it also provides a higher level of confidence for both consumers and staff and reduces unnecessary costs and delays related to corrections or repairs late in the production process.

Maintaining safety in the workplace is an absolute requirement in order to reduce the risk of property loss, personal injury, or death.

Unless every employee is committed to maintaining a customer focus and helping customers wherever they can, the company will never achieve the highest level of customer satisfaction and referral sales.

The risks related to home building can be reduced through insurance and an effective risk management program will include adequate coverage based on the size and scope of the operation.

Local, state, and federal payroll taxes and estimated income taxes must be deposited or paid on time in order to meet financial obligations and maintain a more conservative and predictable cash position.

Following the lead of benchmark companies and creating an advisory board can be very effective methods of reducing risks and increasing the quality of decisions by creating a broader knowledge base.

Maintaining a policy of current pay and taking discounts will not only improve the quality of trade partnerships, help insure best prices, and improve the bottom line, it will also help maintain the integrity of the business plan and provide a safety net in the event of a temporarily tight cash position.

Maintaining adequate working capital is probably the key to minimizing risks and reducing the stress of owning a homebuilding company.

In most cases, home builders become over-leveraged as a result of on-going losses that erode equity. The condition develops after startup and it can destroy the company's ability to secure financing.

Historically, condominium associations have become a vehicle for disgruntled homeowners to gain support for class action litigation with little personal financial exposure.

Critical requirements for the sale of a company include the development of well-conceived business plans, written policies, standardized procedures, the development of effective processes, a high level of customer satisfaction, a reputation for effective management, and a substantial earnings history. These are the same requirements for a successful homebuilding company.

CHAPTER 7

FINANCIAL CONTROLS AND INSOLVENCY

Studies have found that 80 percent new businesses fail in the first five years and more than 50 percent of all business failures occur in the first five years. According to experts, some of the factors that contribute to these failures include the following.

Competition or the inability to compete with others in the critical market area
This is a condition that is substantially reduced through proper planning with the help of marketing consultants.

Insufficient working capital or the failure to recognize the need for proper capitalization, given the scope of activity of the business
A condition that largely results from poor cash management and/or a failure to create an adequate business plan that would identify the need for, and help pursue, sources of equity financing.

Insufficient equity capital in relation to debt or excessive leveraging in order to force growth with limited resources
Again, a condition that typically results from poor planning, a failure to understand and apply proper debt ratios, and/or a failure to raise the capital necessary for expansion or to offset the operating losses in a going concern.

Inadequate sales, often resulting from product decisions, over pricing, poor marketing methods, inadequate sales representation, and/or poor marketing policies
Such a condition can largely be overcome by inviting consultants to participate in the planning and product development processes, being more selective in hiring practices, and using focus groups in order to get closer to the target market.

Improper pricing including pricing too low or too high
Establishing adequate pricing policies (see this chapter) with the right mix of standard and optional features, and developing a market study that includes a detailed survey of the competition will help prevent this problem.

Excessive expenses and cost overruns

Developing policies, procedures, and processes that, among other things, include proper budgeting and financial controls, a quality building program, a partnership program, and a compensation program with performance incentives, will generally control such tendencies.

Poor purchasing policies

Again, this is largely the result of policies, procedures, and processes that lack formality and establish accountability.

Poor policies related to the payment of debt

Inadequate policies related to debt are often the result of an attempt to over-leverage a company without understanding the dynamics of cash flow, debt to equity standards, and/or the need to maintain proper capitalization.

Over investment in fixed assets

Although a decision to build homes on speculation can sometimes produce unavoidable risks that can only be minimized through knowledge of the market and market dynamics, adequate financial planning and proper cash management will generally prevent over investment from becoming the cause of a business failure.

Over expansion

A decision to expand before the proper staffing and planning is in place, and before policy, procedures, and processes have been developed, will generally produce an extraordinary hardship.

Inadequate cash management

A failure to create a well-conceived business plan and cash budget, to monitor progress against the plan, and to understand the principles of cash management, will generally create a basic weakness that can threaten the success of a company.

Operational Influences

These are typically conditions that develop as a result of poor procedures and processes, or they may be both internal and external conditions effecting operations that develop during the course of business, that would normally be anticipated or recognized through pro-active management.

Aging of notes and accounts receivable

Although this generally has little to do with the failure of home building companies, policy should dictate, and good money management requires, that notes and accounts receivable must be collected when due.

Poor collection policies

Policy, procedures, and processes should require the vigorous pursuit of final payments on contracts, the release of escrows, and the collection of other receivables.

Excessive discounting

Home builders must protect their margins and understand that discounting, for any reason, is a bad idea.

An examination of the causes of business failures clearly reveals the need for well focused planning, adequate financing, and effective cash management. By implementing the planning process outlined in this book and then monitoring the variances, home builders can effectively protect their companies from many of the financial conditions that can become fatal. In order to recognize and avoid trouble, business owners and senior managers must instill discipline, implement effective controls, and monitor variances carefully.

FINANCIAL CONTROLS

The responsibility for financial controls in home building companies varies. In small companies, it is typically the responsibility of the owner or president, in a medium-volume company it may be the responsibility of the owner, president, or controller. In large companies it is typically the responsibility of a chief financial officer (CFO) or vice president of finance. For the purpose of presenting information on financial controls, the needs of the large company have been assumed. In small companies, the same needs and level of discipline are required, but it is generally slightly less complicated and provided by someone who is not focused solely on financial management.

Today, financial managers generally have direct responsibility for the financial control process and it has become important for every key manager to understand the theory and practice of financial management. It is also important that financial managers understand that it should be their purpose to support the effort of others and to help them improve through a better understanding of financial dynamics. The role of the financial manager is to:

♦ Initiate the financial planning process

♦ Prepare financial plans

♦ Conduct reviews and adjust financial plans

♦ Maintain financial control and coordinate the efforts of other managers

♦ Participate in investment and financing discussions

♦ Represent the company's interests in money and capital markets

THE PLANNING PROCESS

The planning process is the foundation for all business activity. It results in a business plan that provides the basis for financial control. It is a discipline that forces owners and every senior employee to focus on the requirements for outstanding performance, and it then provides the yardstick by which actual performance will be measured. It establishes the benchmarks and provides the vehicle for variance reporting that is necessary in order to monitor the progress of the company. It enables management by the exception, which gives individual managers an increased capacity to handle volume efficiently. If the planning process is implemented properly, the quality of the business plan will be very good and it will provide an exceptional tool for the growth and development of the company.

When compared to benchmark companies, gross margin can be thought of as the basic measurement of businesses efficiency. In the Income and Expense Comparison table presented in Chapter 3, the difference in gross margin between all of the builders that participated in the study, and the top 25 percent of those builders, was 2.90 percent; on $10 million in revenue, that difference is $290,000 and on $50 million in revenue, it is $1,450,000. In most cases, this is the payoff for extraordinary business management. It generally results from exceptional strategic and financial planning combined with a higher level of management practice, and it permits a level of growth and development that will leverage opportunity. Companies that have a track record for creating well-conceived business plans, executing in conformance with those plans, implementing sound financial controls, and maintaining higher levels of gross margin are rare, but those who have mastered this level of discipline are the ones that attract financial investment and achieve the highest levels of success.

BUDGETS

In the broadest sense, a budget is a comprehensive quantitative plan for the utilization of the resources of a company for some specific period of time. It is an estimate of revenue and expenses over a period of time; a projection of financial conditions with appropriate schedules and forecasts that reflects the plans of an organization over a specific period of time. The budgeting process is important because it provides an opportunity for the exchange of ideas and objectives among people in various departments or with different strengths and weaknesses. Budgets provide a framework for cost awareness, performance evaluation, and they help establish goals and objectives. They can also modify behavior and help create a more meaningful culture; they help create a sense of cooperation and teaming. In order to be effective, budgets must be conservative and realistic.

In most large homebuilding organizations, budgets are prepared by departmental managers and then included into the financial plan for the company. Base budgeting spreadsheets are typically prepared and provided by the financial manger. Such worksheets will include the codes. When they are completed, they will provide the detailed information for each department that will then be incorporated into the financial plan summaries.

THE CASH BUDGET

A *cash budget* is a projection of anticipated cash flows for a given period; sometimes referred to as a cash flow analysis. It is a very important management and planning tool, and most lenders and knowledgeable investors will require it. For home builders, the cash budget is typically a summary of income less disbursements (see Appendix B) for a specific period showing the month-to-month cash flow and accumulated cash balance by month. The basis for such summaries are forecasts of sales, starts, and closings that project current trends using existing data. The cash budget includes estimated operating income as well as income from other sources, and it also includes the projected disbursements of costs and expenses for the various cost categories, as well as the repayment of loans and any required distributions of income to investors or partners.

The cash budget must not be confused with a statement of cash flows which is an accounting statement designed to provide information about the cash receipts and cash payments of a business entity during the accounting period. This statement is also intended to provide information about all of the investing and financing activities of the company during the period. A statement of cash flows is typically included with the income statement and balance sheet at year-end. It is an accounting tool used more for evaluation, while the cash budget is a planning tool used more for management and operations.

Cost accounting assigns book value to assets, which become summarized on the balance sheet. A market-value statement presents those same assets at market value by adjusting the book value of the asset with an offsetting entry to equity. While the market-value statement has no standing as an accounting tool, it is sometimes important to evaluate assets and related debt at market value in anticipation of growth or the sale of a building company.

Positive cash flow may be more important than profitability in a growing company. Nothing can happen or continue to happen without the proper management of money. Growth requires cash and a great deal of it, it fosters a high rate of cost consumption, it provides less time to regenerate cash surpluses, and it poses greater risks to the holders of both debt and equity. A number of companies are profitable as they enter bankruptcy, but they lack the cash to make it work. Without the cash required to fuel the company, the company will break down, and growth becomes a magnifier of this condition.

Understanding the factors that drive cash flow can help every employee grow the business and insure that cash flow remains positive. There are seven drivers of cash flow:

◆ Growth in sales

◆ Improving margins

◆ Controlling operating expenses

◆ Collecting receivables

◆ Minimizing inventory

◆ Controlling payables

◆ Sound capital budgeting

Cash budgets help establish the cash flow planning necessary to insure adequate cash reserves. Once such cash budgets are established, they must be monitored closely, adjustments must be made wherever necessary, and investors, owners, and senior management must acknowledge any future cash demands.

FINANCIAL STATEMENTS

Interim and year-end financial statements are standardized summaries of the performance of a company over a certain period of time. They are important tools for financial control because they summarize the results of actual performance and can highlight significant areas of concern or a need for improvement. The most effective statements are comparative financial statements that provide both a horizontal and vertical analysis for two or more periods. A horizontal analysis compares trends and relationships of items appearing on statements and notes the dollar or percentage change.

*A **horizontal analysis** of financial statements provides a comparison the performance for a particular accounting period (month, quarter or year) against another by recording the $ or % of change from the past period. This is not something that home builders use very often.*

A vertical analysis converts items to a percentage of total assets, liabilities, income, or expenses. Such summaries should be prepared and reviewed monthly, quarterly, and at year-end. They are a snap-shot of the company's performance for a specific period and they are fundamental tools for financial management.

*A **vertical analysis** of financial statements measures line items against total assets, liabilities, income or expenses expressed as a percent of the total. The consolidated income statement for ABC Building in Appendix A is a good example of a vertical analysis; all of the line items are expressed as a percentage of total revenue (or sales).*

Home builders often maintain separate entities for various construction projects in order to limit liability, accommodate separate investment, prevent the co-mingling of funds, provide for separate accounting, and to restrict the amount of company information that may become public knowledge. In these cases, a parent entity usually receives building fees, reimbursements of particular expenses, and profit distributions from the operating entities. In such cases, it is normal and usual to prepare a consolidated income statement and balance sheet that reflect summaries for all of the operating entities as well as the parent.

CONDUCTING AUDITS

In general terms, a financial audit is an activity intended to examine or verify information, procedures, and processes in order to validate accuracy or compliance. There are essentially three types of financial audits:

◆ An audit of financial statements

◆ A special-purpose or compliance audit

◆ An operation audit

Every company should conduct internal audits on a regular basis and large companies, or companies with special needs, should have audits conducted by outside third-party auditors that can certify the results. Internal audits are usually informal and are typically conducted for management purposes only, while external audits are typically conducted in order to demonstrate the quality of financial management through certification.

Often, home builders will fail to understand the importance of a formal internal operational audit. A procedure designed primarily to evaluate the implementation of policy, procedures, and processes established by the company. Such audits are critical to insure compliance in such areas as new project feasibility, land development, purchasing, construction, sales and settlement processing, and warranty service, as well as human resource and financial management. In order to conduct such an audit, policies, procedures, and processes must be clear and contained in written directives. Although such an audit can be an arduous task for an owner or his representative, it can help minimize risks and insure the level of performance that was contemplated in the business plan.

ACCOUNTING STANDARDS

In general, accounting practice is controlled by industry standards and the requirement for the certification of public accountants. Companies must maintain accounting systems that conform to the rules that govern accounting practice and the preparation of financial statements known as the *Generally Accepted Accounting Practices (GAAP)*. They must also rely on certified public accountants that are either employed by the company, who provide services for a fee, or both. Maintaining the quality of accounting information is a legal requirement and it is essential for the proper evaluation of financial information.

DIRECT COST ESTIMATING

Direct cost estimating systems for home building are generally based on the collection and presentation of *direct cost* line items, phases, group phases, and various cost summaries. In most cases, a unit-cost database is established, updated periodically, and used in the formulas for the extension of each item in the cost projection. Quantities are taken off of the plans manually and entered on spreadsheets, or by a digitizer, which enters the measurements automatically and the computer then calculates the quantities based on predefined formulas. Once the quantities have been taken off and the extensions of unit costs have been made, those extensions are presented on a spreadsheet and in summaries that can be obtained for various reports. Part of the beauty of using a computer program for estimating is the power of a work-package takeoff. Work-package takeoff allows the estimator to create automatic extensions of a particular measurement for various items in different phases; the estimator can take off the lineal footage of an interior wall once, and as an extension, distribute costs and quantities to interior stud and plate, drywall (both sides of the wall), wood base molding, nails, painting, etc. Once the cost estimate is complete, summaries can be automatically transferred to job-cost budgets if an integrated computer software system exists. Such estimating is powerful and inexpensive when you consider the enormous advantage over manual or basic spreadsheet methods.

Estimating can be a substantial source of risk for new or growing builders. Estimating errors can result in losses or a substantially reduced profit margin. Some costs that are often missed by a new estimator include those related to vandalism and theft, sales taxes, and omissions and errors. Each of these categories represents costs, or potential costs, of a project and must be included in the estimates. Vandalism and theft should be based on reasonable expectations or experience. Sales taxes should be applied to materials as they are taken off, included in the unit pricing, or they should be applied as an add-on after the takeoff and estimates are complete, The omissions and errors category should be based on historical information, or, it should be the result of a careful evaluation of experience, estimating procedure, and industry standards (it will typically range between .75 and 1.50 percent of total costs). Any failure to include these items in a cost estimate will effectively reduce profits.

Once direct cost estimates have been prepared, the phase totals (which are established by grouping a large number of related estimating items) are transferred and maintained in job-cost records, as budget phase and group phase totals, which create the total budget for a single unit. As purchase orders for labor, material, and equipment are approved for payment, coded, and paid, the total costs are posted to the job cost records and maintained by the same phase and group phase classifications as costs-to-date for a particular house or construction project.

JOB COST ACCOUNTING

The function of job-cost accounting is to provide information related to the actual costs for categories established by both budgets and estimates, in order to produce variance reports. All payments are coded and posted to the job cost records using a format that is consistent with the original budgets and estimates. Job cost reports are typically run at the end-of-month and end-of-quarter in order to provide management with comparisons of actual costs-to-date against the budget and estimate totals that were part of the business plan. The complete cost control system is based on a periodic measurement of actual costs against the estimated costs to produce variances in order to establish accountability. Such reports typically become the subject of major quarterly cost reviews that should include discussions of performance against the business plan among owners and senior management. Each variance must be examined carefully and should force some action on the part of management. Adjustments of estimates and budgets, improvements in a process, or changes in operating procedures are just some of the typical responses to variance reporting.

There are a number of back-office business systems created to help home builders monitor job costs. Today, these systems have become very sophisticated and powerful software applications that often operate in a seamless environment with other applications such as accounting, accounts payable, payroll, sales management, design collaboration, estimating, purchasing, and warranty-service management. Each application is an important part of the overall building process and the reports that are generated by such programs are invaluable. Job cost reports are a critical part of maintaining profitability. Typically, they list budgeted costs that have been loaded from the business plan, they summarize actual costs incurred, and they report the variances to date. In cases where costs are less, the variance if favorable and in cases where costs are greater, the variance is unfavorable and will have a negative effect on projected income.

Requiring accountability for costs is a critical part of financial management and it is particularly critical for homebuilding companies because of the complicated nature of their cost structures. In large companies, the responsibility for costs is departmentalized by department heads and incorporated into the forecasts reflected in the business plan. Costs to date are then monitored by cost code and variance reports are generated and reviewed by senior managers. Each manager will depend on the other to manage the costs generated by their department. Where significant variations occur (both favorable and unfavorable), they should be discusses, adjusted if possible, or acknowledged as an ongoing variance either overlooked in the planning process or resulting from actual conditions that cannot be altered. Unfavorable variances or variances that effect the profitability of the business plan in a negative way must be monitored carefully. Actual results may be formally reviewed against plan on a quarterly basis and a new forecast will be rolled up at mid-year and adjusted again at year-end in order to create the new business plan for the following year. This process of budgetary control and variance reporting will continue for the life of the project in order to insure the highest level of profitability for the project and to provide critical financial information for the management of the company.

MANAGEMENT REPORTING

Management reporting of financial information should occur routinely on a monthly, quarterly, and annual basis. Such information should include the cost variance reports for each entity together with and end-of-month, end-of-quarter, and end-of-year financial statements. In addition to formal quarterly budget review meetings, senior staff should include significant variances on the agenda of regularly scheduled monthly meetings. Monitoring the performance against plan is critical and should remain a focus of senior management.

Status reporting should occur weekly for sales, production, and warranty service in order to provide critical information that may have an impact on the future financial performance of the company and its ability to achieve plan goals. The overall performance of the team is dependent on the performance of each team member and his department. Such reporting provides the critical information necessary for each member to evaluate operating conditions that may have an effect on their performance, and it enables the management team to support one another in their efforts. In the event that variances are considerable, business plans may require updating more frequent than quarterly with a reforecast at mid-year.

Many financial managers and department heads routinely distribute such key management information by email. In other cases, the company maintains a confidential compartmentalized drive on the server where such reports are posted with limited access for owners and senior managers. Because of the importance of the weekly operating reports for work-in-process (production), sales and settlements, and warranty service, many home builders are posting such reports on restricted Internet sites for use by staff, trade contractors, suppliers, lenders, and investors.

PURCHASE ORDERS

A purchase order is a formal written document used for financial control that authorizes and initiates the purchase of labor, material, equipment, or services. In some cases, these documents are automatically produced by computers and printers following a release to production. They often serve as a payment authorization when they are approved by a construction manager indicating that the work has been completed and that it is acceptable; in such cases, the purchase order is used by vendors in lieu of traditional invoicing. Purchase orders are an absolute requirement for any company building more than one hundred houses per year and they are strongly recommended for any company building more than fifty. No home building company can grow and develop without an effective purchase order system. Purchase orders offer the following advantages for home builders:

◆ They restate the labor, material, equipment, or services to be purchased.

◆ They help control costs by paying in accordance with contracts.

◆ They protect against duplicate payments.

◆ They permit management by the exception; a key concept for anyone building volume.

A *variance purchase order* (VPO) is a purchase order for labor, material, equipment, or a service that is not under contract or included in budgets and therefore, the purchase constitutes a variance from plan. The use of VPOs will call attention to the additional costs and create a red flag for management. Such documents can help management deal with unfavorable cost variances immediately in order to preserve the integrity of the plan or the quality of financial reporting. They may also be used for non-standard options where there are no provisions in labor and material contracts, specifications, or payment schedules.

MANAGING BANK RELATIONSHIPS

Obtaining lenders should be the result of a very carefully orchestrated process. They have been targeted, some have been the result of power referrals, and the company has gone to great expense to establish a business relationship that will serve the needs of one or more projects. It is the responsibility of financial managers to protect and extend those relationships on behalf of the company. Communication is very important and honesty in reporting is critical in order to protect the interests of the company. The financial manager should schedule periodic "wellness meetings" with loan officers on a regular basis. These meetings should include an exchange of business reports and financial statements as well as a discussion of current conditions, challenges, and opportunities for the project. Keep in mind that few people are as well qualified as bankers to provide financial advise.

Bankers are generally expert negotiators; it is a prerequisite for their success. In order to negotiate or improve loan terms and conditions up front, a builder must be in a good market and have an excellent record of performance. As unbelievable as it may seem, borrowers can generally negotiate better deals when a loan is in jeopardy. At those times, bankers are more willing to make concessions that will lead to the preservation of the loan principle. Interest rate reductions, extensions of terms, and/or the postponement of payments all have positive implications for current cash flows and are often used by lenders to provide support for troubled borrowers. Often, the key to success here is open and honest communication combined with a well-conceived plan of action.

USING RESERVES TO CONTROL INCOME

Reserve accounts are one of the most subjective areas of financial reporting because company executives, rather than accountants and financial managers generally establish them, and they are estimates of future requirements. Reserve accounts are generally the focus of auditors, but usually only when the company is in some trouble. Some home builders have used reserves for service and other items to structure income. In very profitable years, they have inflated such reserves and in less profitable years, they have understated such reserves in order to improve revenue figures. This type of income manipulation is a dangerous practice and it is a violation of a trust for financial managers should look for. The basis for any reserve should be well documented and acknowledged by the owners and responsible managers of the company. In cases of real financial liability, reserves are appropriate and desirable, but they should reflect the best judgment of the company and not be used to control income. The basis for establishing any reserve should be preserved in a written document for future auditors.

OTHER FINANCIAL CONTROLS

Some other financial controls or policies employed by home builders in order to insure a higher level of performance against the plan include:

Check Signers
In order to insure accuracy and to protect against dishonesty, companies should require that any two or more officers or designees sign checks.

Certificates of Insurance
Unless a certificate of insurance can be provided to insurance auditors for trade contractors, the builder will be responsible for the cost of their basic coverage based on payments made to the contractor. In order to protect the company from this liability, current certificates of insurance must be required and monitored in order to complete the vendor records.

Lien Releases
Many jurisdictions provide mechanics lien rights for trade contractors in order to insure proper payment. In those jurisdictions, it is imperative that trade contractors acknowledge payment and the release of any lien rights that have been paid. In those cases, home builders should require the execution of a certificate that acknowledges receipt of payment and the release of any lien rights on paid properties.

Bank Reconciliation
Cash accounts should be reconciled promptly in order to insure the quality of accounting information.

Ratio Analysis

Significant ratios should be calculated automatically and included on all financial reports. This will help owners and senior managers become more aware of the financial health of their businesses. This is particularly true of leverage ratios that can help measure the balance between debt and equity.

Closing Deadlines

It is in the best interest of the company to close the books as quickly as possible following the end of the month. Policy should require that the books are closed and accounting statements are provided by the 15th of the following month unless it is a year-end closing which will require considerably more time. This will provide timely management tools that are necessary to assess performance levels and it will help generate enthusiasm where the statements reflect performance that is substantially in conformance with the plan.

Duplicate Payments

Duplicate payments are a particular problem for small builders who operate without the benefit of purchase orders or a strong back-office accounts payable system. Unless there is some failsafe system to prevent duplicate payments, the probability of a duplicate payment increases considerably with volume. It is not uncommon for a trade contractor to bill more than once for the same item, or for internal confusion to result in a duplicate payment.

Endorsement Statements

Often statements are written above the endorsement block or on the face of a check in order to secure an acknowledgement by the endorser of the check in order to protect the financial interests of a company. An example of such an endorsement that could be used in order to require the endorser to acknowledge that a payment is in full and to eliminate the possibility of a future dispute over additional charges might be:

> *"This check constitutes full and final payment for all labor and material related to the construction of Lot 12, Block A, of the Grubby Thicket Subdivision."*

Although such endorsements may be challenged in court, they offer additional proof of the intent of the parties at the time of payment and deposit.

Two Party Checks

Two party checks are sometimes used in order to protect against claims by a third party. This is particularly true in jurisdictions with mechanic lien laws, when a trade contractor, providing labor and material, has not paid the supplier for the material delivered to and used in the construction of a particular property. Where furnish and install contracts are used, it is important that the builder be aware of the payment performance of the vendor. Although the trade contractor may object to this, it is the best way to insure payment for the material in order to avoid a possible lien in the future.

Respect for Creditors

Benchmark companies typically maintain a culture that demonstrates respect for creditors. They maintain strong lines of communication, they are pro-active regarding their responsibilities, and they make every reasonable effort to accommodate creditors where they can.

MAINTAINING PROFITABILITY

PRICING

New or less sophisticated home builders have a tendency to establish prices based on costs plus a standard mark-up. Unfortunately, cost-based pricing formulas create opportunities for both under-pricing and over-pricing. Keep in mind that margin is calculated against sales price and cost-based pricing is a markup against costs; a 25 percent markup on cost is only a 20 percent margin on sales price. Unless you are a custom home builder, building one-of-a-kind homes on competitive bid contracts, you may want to consider the alternative.

The builder must first establish what the market will pay for the home that the company intends to build. If the company starts with a market study that includes a competitive analysis, it can then convert those facts to an architectural design and specifications that will satisfy the anticipated market target and capture the market share that is anticipated. This approach should then reveal the velocity that is likely and permit the builder to mobilize a production capacity to meet the anticipated demand. By working backward from the market price with reasonable costs, the builder will ultimately determine what the company can afford to pay for the ground. This is the exercise that must be performed during the feasibility analysis for a new project.

Every home builder should consider velocity carefully. In the event that he or she is not able to handle the anticipated velocity, he or she may want to assume a high margin, low inventory turn strategy. Most high volume home builders, however, will opt for high velocity. They might rather accept a 5 percent margin with a 30 percent return on investment (ROI) if they can get in and out quickly. The anticipated velocity on a project is largely a result of an evaluation of the facts contained in a market study, the experience of staff, and the production capacity of the company.

Once base and standard option prices have been set, the builder must monitor sales carefully. In the event that sales are softer than anticipated, it may be wise to offer option incentives in order to help stimulate initial sales. In the event that sales are stronger than anticipated, a very carefully conceived price increase strategy should probably be developed. Every new project should be opened for sales with a price increase strategy in order to cover the possibility that sales will be stronger than anticipated. At the end of the day, the market will pay for the perceived value they see in the product and their decision will have nothing at all to do with cost.

SALES AND SETTLEMENT ACTIVITY

Sales are the lifeblood of any building company and a successful sales program is a requirement for continued operation; operating income is the direct result of sales and settlements. In order to insure success, sales and settlement activity must be monitored carefully and adjusted where necessary. Sales and traffic reports are critical, and traffic surveys can help identify areas that require well-focused attention. In the event that sales are softer than anticipated, the builder must examine the conditions and determine why the actual results does not agree with the economic model. It could be an error in the planning process, a condition resulting from inadequate execution, or both. By monitoring traffic counts and actual contracts, a conversion rate can be calculated and compared to historical performance in order to help determine whether the problem is on-site (sales staff, product, or merchandising) or if it is related to the location, marketing effort, local economy, or some other external factor.

Most successful home builders will examine the assumptions first and then evaluate the current sales and marketing program. Often, home builders will require that on-site sales managers have a track record of considerable success in order to further insure that the agent will not be the likely reason for poor sales. They will also hire one or more marketing consultants to shop their jobs in order to obtain third-party evaluations of their sales program. Once the facts are in, thoughtful action can be taken to improve the condition. In cases where absorption is substantially less than that which was anticipated by the plan, the plan must be revised and operational adjustments must be made in order to insure an acceptable level of performance.

Sales processing includes a wide range of activities necessary to ratify the contract and prepare the purchaser for closing. In order to assure that the closing will occur upon the completion of construction, a series of steps must be taken and monitored. The contract must be ratified, options and material selections must be made by the purchaser, loan application must be made, contingencies must be removed in some cases, a qualification letter must be obtained from the lender, a written loan commitment must obtained, the closing must be scheduled with both an attorney and the buyer, the buyer must be notified in writing and given instructions, instructions must be sent to the closing attorney, and provisions must be made for the disbursement of funds. It is a process that requires constant monitoring in large companies and, unless it is managed properly, delays will occur that will effect customer satisfaction, profitability, and cash flow.

CONSTRUCTION PROGRESS

Residential construction is a complicated process that functions substantially without the benefit of controlled conditions. The exposure to unpredictable weather conditions and a semi-skilled work force have more to do with maintaining schedules and construction quality than most people realize. In many markets, the trade professionals serving the housing industry lack the skill and professionalism of those serving the commercial markets. Commercial contractors generally pay more and single-structure-construction represents far better working conditions than the scattered lot construction of most residential projects. In most highly competitive markets, labor is scarce and builders compete with one another for the tradesmen with the highest skill levels.

From a management standpoint, the most critical elements of the construction program are start time, the quality of construction, and the overall build- or cycle-time. Unless the construction department is able to pull the permits and start new homes in accordance with the timeline established by the business plan, they will not be able to maintain projected completion dates. Unless construction managers are able to maintain high standards of construction, costs will typically increase, customer satisfaction will diminish, and profitability will be impacted. Unless construction managers are able to maintain the cycle-time established by the business plan, costs will increase, customer satisfaction will suffer, profitability will be impacted, and cash will not flow as planned.

For these reasons, home builders must constantly monitor construction starts, quality, and build-time. It is critical that each of these components occur as planned. In most cases a single management report is generated weekly that monitors start dates, work in progress, and anticipated completion dates. Unless these critical element work in concert with sales and settlement priorities, the level of performance reflected in the business plan will not be met. Business plans must reflect conservative thinking and most successful builders and senior sales and construction managers will attempt to exceed the performance established by the business plan. Nothing will do more for the morale of the production department (both construction and purchasing departments) in a large public company, than starting the last house scheduled for delivery in a fiscal year knowing that its completion before year-end is a slam-dunk.

PERFORMANCE INCENTIVES

Recruiting, training, and developing a building team is a costly and difficult task. In most cases, it involves some degree of performance management of poor performers or those who threaten the culture. Once these employees have become strong contributing members of the team, they must be protected and encouraged to achieve higher standards of performance. Maintaining a compensation program that includes a competitive base salary, goal oriented performance bonuses for general employees, and profit sharing incentives for senior managers will do more to improve productivity, promote teambuilding, and improve profitability than anything else a builder could do. Senior employees in exceptional companies should be allowed to share in the financial success of the business and every employee should have the opportunity to increase his compensation as a result of exceptional performance.

By establishing competitive base salaries with performance incentives, the employer is committed only to the base salary. Anything above base salary will depend on the employee's contribution or the success of the business. In depressed markets, this means that the base salary for the senior staff is the fallback position when net income may be marginal. The fortunes of owners and senior managers should rise and fall with the success of the company and general staff should probably have the opportunity to be fairly rewarded for their above average contribution in any market condition.

INVOLVE THE COMPANY

Companies, both large and small, should enable employees and invite them to participate in the planning and review process. Summaries of the plan should be shared openly with the entire staff prior to adoption, and each employee should be invited to provide input through his senior manager. Quarterly meetings with a carefully constructed agenda designed to inform employees, evaluate actual performance against the plan, and encourage participation will do a great deal to help maintain a strong sense of team. Such meetings can be extremely successful when combined with strong dynamic leadership. They typically create enthusiasm, inspire meaningful input, and improve morale.

USING SURVEYS AND FOCUS GROUPS

Well-conceived surveys of attitudes related to the products and the operations of building companies are excellent resources for improvement. They can provide meaningful information that can be used in the planning process and they can help management find ways to increase revenue and reduce costs. A typical homeowner satisfaction survey might measure attitudes toward design, building materials, quality of construction, the marketing program, the sales and sales processing program, and production, as well as sales, construction, and service staff. Surveys might also be used with trade contractors to encourage them to help improve the building process by evaluating current designs, materials, policies and procedures, construction quality, and construction management procedures. The value of each survey will be determined by the quality of the questions, the level of response, and the tabulation and reporting. Each survey should be designed with specific measurements in mind; the referral rate resulting from homeowner satisfaction surveys should be a critical focal point for improvement.

Focus groups can provide a great deal of information that has the potential of improving the business by increasing revenue or reducing costs. Typically, focus groups are used to evaluate product during the development stage or to validate the effectiveness of the sales and/or warranty service processes. Such groups can be assembled in either a formal or informal setting, but each will require a facilitator, a list of prepared standardized questions, and written records that document the results.

PARTNERSHIP MEETINGS

Partnership meetings provide excellent opportunities to communicate directly with those who have the most impact on the production process and cycle-time. It affords the opportunity to provide information related to the future of the company, to reinforce policies and processes, to present production goals, to reward outstanding performance, to discuss areas of concern, to emphasize the need for safety in the workplace, and to facilitate pro-active customer care. It is also an excellent opportunity to solicit the support of vendors in the implementation of financial plans. Much of the financial management is dependent on a level of production that has been established by the plan. Cycle-time or build-time has been established in the plan based on the expectations of management and it controls the cash flow cycle for home builders. If cycle-time can be reduced through improved performance, it will typically improve profitability and cash flow for both the vendors and the home builder; a win, win situation.

PROTECTING THE COMPANY

Due to the sophistication and complexities of housing markets, home builders must manage their businesses carefully and create cash strategies that will protect their companies during times of turbulence, distress, or change. Understanding what influences might threaten the success of the company, and then developing contingency plans to deal with them, will insure a more predictable outcome. Some actions that can help a company prepare for trouble or change include:

◆ Increase equity when the company is healthy and performing well.

◆ Maintain higher levels of cash reserves in short-tern investments.

◆ Build and hold some homes for rental that can be sold in order to book income in slow markets.

◆ Build income producing property in order to create alternative sources of income and create assets that can be sold down the road.

◆ Develop alternative sources of capital before you need them.

◆ Develop profit centers that require less cash and credit such as custom homes and major renovations.

◆ Diversify by acquiring a business that will not be affected when the housing market is soft.

◆ Provide truck and auto allowances rather that providing trucks and autos for employees.

INSOLVENCY

Insolvency results from the inability of a debtor to pay financial obligations as they mature. In its worse case, insolvency is a condition where the liabilities of a debtor exceed the fair market value of its assets. Such a condition often leads to a bankruptcy, which is a formal proceeding initiated voluntarily by a financially troubled debtor, or involuntarily by creditors when the debtor is generally not paying debts as they become due. A condition that requires the filing of a petition in a federal court under the Bankruptcy Code, which is a federal statute that provides the basis for the federal bankruptcy system in effect today. Generally speaking, bankruptcies lead to either a formal court directed reorganization, or liquidation.

A cash flow crisis, insolvency, and the possibility of bankruptcy all result from a builder's failure or inability to recognize, evaluate, and adjust to the internal and external forces that drive his business. It should be apparent by now that such conditions can be avoided through:

◆ Careful strategic and financial planning.

◆ A well-disciplined pursuit of planning goals and objectives.

◆ Careful and continuous monitoring of actual performance related to those plans.

◆ On-going evaluation of both internal and external forces effecting operations.

◆ Interim adjustments to short-term planning.

◆ Annual re-evaluation and formal revisions of both strategic and financial planning.

CAUSES OF INSOLVENCY

In many cases, insolvency is the first stage of a business failure. Some of the most common causes of insolvency include the following:

◆ Soft market conditions

◆ Inadequate working capital

◆ Improper use of working capital

◆ Inadequate financing

◆ Delayed funding of loans

◆ Delayed progress and final payments

◆ Cost overruns

◆ Excessive leverage

◆ Embezzlement

◆ Judgments

Most large home builders are not often guilty of poor financial management. They use financial advisors and they employ a chief financial officer to help develop and monitor financial strategies. On the other hand, small- and medium-volume builders, who build less than 100 units per year, are often guilty of poor financial management, particularly in the first five years. Poor financial management has been the fatal error that has resulted in insolvency and bankruptcy.

RECOVERING FROM INSOLVENCY

No one wins in a bankruptcy. Home builders, who find themselves approaching a cash crisis or who have become insolvent, must try to reorganize debt and identify an out-of-court workout. Most debtors will help if a plan of reorganization is fair and communicated with confidence. The basic requirements for any business recovery are:

◆ To acknowledge the problem

◆ Get advice

◆ Develop a plan

◆ Stimulate sales

◆ Eliminate the toys

◆ Cut quickly and deeply

◆ Restructure debt

◆ Convert assets to cash

◆ Focus on strength

Many of the requirements for an effective plan of recovery are those same requirements that have been outlined in this book for effective planning, financing, and cash management. Anyone facing insolvency should reread this book and begin to implement the planning, policy, procedures, processes, and general management practice presented.

SUMMARY STATEMENT

There is no substitute for working within a process that reduces risks and provides an ongoing opportunity to understand the dynamics of the business and its affect on the financial condition of the company. Effective planning, financing, and cash management will provide the foundation for the growth and development of a homebuilding business. It will give the company the ability to achieve long-term goals and to take advantage of market opportunities along the way. Keep in mind that the process of planning, financing, and cash management is dynamic and it is an ongoing process. To be effective, these critical activities must continue to be a priority and a constant focus of both owners and senior managers.

CHAPTER SUMMARY

Studies have found that four out of five new businesses fail in the first five years and more than 50 percent of all business failures occur in the first five years.

The role of the financial manager is to: (1) initiate the financial planning process, (2) prepare financial plans, (3) to conduct reviews and adjust financial plans, (4) to maintain financial control and coordinate the efforts of other managers, (5) to participate in investment and financing discussions, and (6) to represent the company's interests in money and capital markets.

When it is compared to benchmark companies, gross margin can be thought of as the basic measurement of businesses efficiency.

A budget is an estimate of revenue and expenses over a period of time; a projection of financial statements with appropriate schedules and forecasts that reflects the plans of an organization over a specific period of time.

A cash budget is a projection of anticipated cash flows for a given period; sometimes referred to as a cash flow analysis.

There are seven drivers of cash flow: 1) growth in sales, 2) improving margins, 3) controlling operating expenses, 4) collecting receivables, 5) minimizing inventory, 6) controlling payables, and 7) sound capital budgeting.

Interim and year-end financial statements are standardized summaries of the performance of a company over a certain period of time.

In general terms, a financial audit is an activity intended to examine or verify information, procedures, and processes in order to validate accuracy or compliance. There are essentially three types of financial audits: (1) an audit of financial statements, (2) a special-purpose or compliance audit, and (3) an operation audit.

The rules that govern accounting practice and the preparation of financial statements known as the Generally Accepted Accounting Practices (GAAP).

The function of job-cost accounting is to provide information related to the actual costs for categories established by both budgets and estimates, in order to produce variance reports.

Cost-based pricing formulas create opportunities for both under-pricing and over-pricing. The builder must first establish what the market will pay; by working backward from the market price with reasonable costs, the builder will ultimately determine what the company can afford to pay for the ground. At the end of the day, the market will pay for the perceived value they see in the product and their decision will have nothing at all to do with cost.

From a management standpoint, the most critical elements of the construction program are start time, the quality of construction, and the overall build- or cycle-time.

Some actions that can help a company prepare for trouble or change include the following:

◆ Increase equity when the company is healthy and performing well.
◆ Maintain higher levels of cash reserves in short-tern investments.
◆ Build and hold some homes for rental, that can be sold in order to book income in slow markets.
◆ Build income producing property in order to create alternative sources of income and create assets that can be sold down the road.
◆ Develop alternative sources of capital before you need them.
◆ Develop profit centers that require less cash and credit such as custom homes and major renovations.
◆ Diversify by acquiring a business that will not be affected when the housing market is soft.
◆ Provide truck and auto allowances rather that providing trucks and autos for employees.

Anyone facing insolvency should reread this book and begin to implement the planning, policy, procedures, processes and general management practice presented.

APPENDICES

A A LONG-TERM PLAN FOR GROWTH AND DEVELOPMENT   121

B A SAMPLE FINANCING PROPOSAL   143

C NAHB CHART OF ACCOUNTS   147

APPENDIX A

A LONG-TERM PLAN FOR GROWTH AND DEVELOPMENT

Appendix A includes a business plan that has been prepared for presentation. The ABC Building Company, Inc., its ownership, investors, advisors, and employees are fictitious and do not exist. This company has been created in the mind of the author to serve as an example of a relatively new home building company with above-average management practice. In this case, the author has created a corporation doing business in various entities for each project. Projects are built and marketed in the name of the parent for fixed building fees that are paid as work progresses. Projects are typically organized as either LLCs or limited partnerships with residual profits passing through either to the parent corporation, or to the original stockholders in the case an LLC. Projects are often funded with separate investment, always controlled by separate accounting, each entity enters into its own labor and material and new home sales contracts, and each entity files its own tax returns.

For the purpose of demonstration, the Company has a two-year history and has just modified its original business plan for the second time. The Company is owned by three individuals including:

(1) an initial owner/president who is middle aged with a good reputation and a solid history in housing
(2) an investor/advisor who is somewhat older than the president and, himself, owns a large, successful land development company
(3) an investor/father-in-law who is retired and is not active in the Company. Both investors are sophisticated and have purchased $100,000 of stock each, at a cost that was twice that of the owner.

The initial owner/president has agreed to guarantee loans, leases, and the like, as long as it is necessary and it is understood that the other two stockholders will not guarantee the debts of the Company.

THE ABC BUILDING COMPANY, INC.
A STRATEGIC AND FINANCIAL PLAN
FOR THE NEXT FIVE YEARS

OPENING THE DOOR TO THE FUTURE

THE EXECUTIVE SUMMARY

The ABC Building Company, Inc. is a two-year old start-up company with its principle office in Rockville, Maryland and various construction projects located in Montgomery County in Maryland and Fairfax County in Virginia. Since its incorporation in March of 2000, the Company has established itself as a medium-volume builder of quality custom homes and up-scale production homes in new communities. Custom homes have been built and sold both on speculation as well as under contracts with lot owners. Production homes are typically built on speculation and under contract in a number of communities.

Volume has steadily increased from twelve houses in the first year of operations to fifty-two in the second year and the Company expects to deliver 85 homes in 2002. Operating revenues have grown from $7.3 million in the year 2000 to $18.8 last year and are expected to reach $31.8 million in 2002; this would undoubtedly place the Company with the top 400 builders in the Country based on revenue. The Company is in the process of substantially increasing its volume and expanding its operations to include land development.

The general philosophy of the current ownership and management of this company has been to limit activity, growth, and market penetration during the first three years in order to reduce risks while becoming more knowledgeable about land positions, acquiring land inventories, establishing financial strength, developing suitable sources of supply, and developing the management team and organization necessary to expand markets and market activities. Now that a solid foundation exists, the Company is ready to accelerate growth and development. The gradual organization and development of this business has been based on the demand measured in niche markets located in the Mid-Atlantic region with an initial emphasis on Montgomery County in the state of Maryland, and Fairfax County in the state of Virginia. Having completed two of the three start-up years, the Company expects to complete its third year with modest growth and then to accelerate growth and development in the last four years covered by this plan.

The strategic and financial planning presented in this summary reflects the varied experience and background that each investor and the initial management team bring to the table. Each member of the team is bound by a desire to develop a strong concept, theme, and management style that will set a new direction in this fiercely competitive industry. A fully integrated concept covers everything from site selection and product development to post-settlement warranty service; a management template that includes the effective planning, policy, procedures, and processes that are requirements for successful high-volume home building. This plan summary has been compiled after careful consideration, debate, and modification; it reflects the combined thinking of the current ownership, management, and advisors of the Company and it will continue to be altered or modified annually based on experience, opportunity, and both the internal and external forces producing change.

STATEMENT OF PURPOSE

The ABC Building Company is a high-end production home builder with a customer focus, and a commitment to quality construction and pro-active customer care. The purpose of the Company is to provide income for employees, return on investment, and to accumulate modest financial growth by measuring demand for a variety of residential construction projects and filling that demand for the benefit of its purchasers and owners; to seek opportunity by evaluating facts, to establish a well-conceived plan of action, and to execute that plan in such a way that its management skill, concern for employees, commitment to the customer, and regard for existing neighborhoods are all obvious. The Company will:

◆ Be ethical in all matters and attempt to resolve disputes based on what is fair, reasonable, and in the best interest of the community.

◆ Protect the environment and conserve natural resources wherever possible and at all reasonable costs.

◆ Cooperate with state and local governments to protect the interests of the public.

◆ Demonstrate concern for production quality and job-site safety.

◆ Encourage employee participation and offer opportunities for self-improvement and an improved quality of life.

◆ Maintain a professional bearing and participate in community affairs and the affairs of the home building industry.

◆ Make every reasonable attempt to provide exceptional customer service, satisfy the demands of our purchasers and owners, and protect their interests wherever possible.

◆ Make every reasonable effort to pay its bills promptly and discount wherever possible.

◆ Attempt to seek innovative solutions to design, engineering, and management problems except where increased risks seem to outweigh the potential benefits of such innovation.

The goal of The ABC Building Company is to build homes that reflect fine architectural and finish detail, to maintain a quality production process, and to provide proactive customer care. The Company will accomplish these goals in following ways:

◆ Inviting accountability

◆ Incorporating uncompromising quality in everything that it does

◆ Creating value through a balance of location, product, price and customer support

◆ Setting expectations for customers and then exceeding those expectations

◆ Instilling and reinforcing confidence in the Company with customers and trade partners

◆ Maintaining a culture that promotes positive relationships with customers and respect for every employee

◆ Promoting a balanced life for employees

THE ORGANIZATION

The ABC Building Company is a standard C corporation, chartered in the state of Maryland in 2000, and domesticated in the state of Virginia in that same year. The Corporation actively builds on its own and is the general partner in two Joint Ventures and three LLCs that have been organized to control activity and limit liability on large construction projects. Having worked in the housing industry for more than twenty years, the President of the Company has considerable experience and influence in the local housing market. He has worked with the Brian Bedford, the current Vice President of Operations, for more than ten years while employed by two other companies. Mr. Smith has committed his resources to the development of the business and expects to grow the business to a level where the Company is a significant force in the Mid-Atlantic region. In a very short period of time, the Company has been able to secure both the land positions and capital investment required to meet its planning goals.

The Company expects to continue this phase of its growth and development through the creation of joint ventures, limited partnerships, and limited liability companies. The Company will continue to build using the parent corporate entity as long as the required capital is available. In cases where it perceives a slightly higher level of risks or in the event that the Company is unable to provide the required capital for a specific development, it will offer such opportunities to sophisticated investors or other companies with the ability to make the investment. In all cases, either the Company or Mr. Smith will retain the control and majority interest in such joint ventures, limited partnerships, or limited liability companies.

OWNERSHIP AND CAPITALIZATION

The start-up capital required for the ABC Building Company, Inc. has been provided solely through the sale of stock. The initial stock offering was limited to a small select group of individuals including William C. Smith (200,000 shares), the current president, Robert D. Jones (50,000 shares), a director and advisor to the Company, and John P. Doe (50,000 shares), a private investor. These three individuals will retain total ownership in the Company until the years 2003 and 2005, when additional stock will be offered to staff and sold to private investors in order to raise additional capital for growth and development. After full dilution in the year 2005, William Smith will still own the controlling interest with 53 percent of the shares outstanding and the initial stockholders collectively will control 79 percent of the authorized and outstanding stock.

CURRENT AND PROPOSED STOCK ISSUE	
	Shares
Current	
Initial Offering	300,000
Proposed	
2003 Capitalization	40,000
2005 Capitalization	40,000
Total Authorized	380,000

THE CULTURE

The ownership and senior management of the Company recognize that the culture of the Company is largely the result of its attitudes, actions, and written directives. The Company has worked hard to establish a unique culture and it will continue to promote a culture based on the following:

◆ Honest and ethical behavior

◆ A professional bearing

◆ A quality building program

◆ Maintaining a customer focus

◆ An open, supportive work environment with real concern for personal development and the quality of life for its employees

◆ Hiring and training employees who are professional, respectful, and courteous to one another at all times

◆ Compensating employees based on performance and contribution

◆ Providing written policies, procedures, and processes that enable employees

◆ Maintaining a high level of efficiency and productivity

◆ Maintaining a safe workplace

◆ Paying bills promptly and discounting wherever possible

◆ Demonstrating respect and concern for those with whom the Company does business

◆ Demonstrating concern for the communities within which the Company builds

◆ Applying standards uniformly and fairly

◆ Resolving complaints and disputes based on what is fair and reasonable

PROFIT CENTERS

Although the Company has a history of building custom homes, it is currently active in a single profit center; production homes in new communities. The Company has established a reputation for production housing with a custom touch, offering a wide range of both standard and non-standard options. Over the next five years, the Company will establish similar production programs in both Howard and Frederick Counties in the state of Maryland and Jefferson County in the state of West Virginia. Expansion into new markets will depend largely on the land opportunities available. In addition to its production activity, the Company expects to reestablish itself as a custom home builder over the next five years. The long-term planning for the Company provides for two profit centers; production housing in new communities and custom homes on scattered lots in smaller communities.

THE PRODUCTS

The Company has developed a large-lot single-family detached product that it calls its Cambridge Series, and it is currently working on a small-lot single-family detached program that it calls its Manchester Series. In addition to the two single-family detached programs, the Company has also created a townhouse program that it calls its Portsmouth Series. All three of these product lines have been developed using a design team that includes staff, a marketing consultant, and three different architects. These three product offerings have also been validated through focus groups and represent broad based appeal in markets ranging from a $275,000 townhouse to an $825,000 semi-custom home.

Current Product

The Cambridge Series consists of six models each ranging in base square footage from 3,400 sq. ft. to 5,000 sq. ft., each with three elevations and a number of optional features designed to expand the size of the home. Options on this program include porches, side sunrooms, kitchen bumps, lofts, and three-car garage.

The Portsmouth Series is a mixed unit product with 24 foot wide two-car garage end units, 22 foot wide single car garage interior units, and interior non-garage back-to-back interior units that are 38 feet by 20 feet. This series is an alley product that features architectural elevations on both front and rear with units that are staggered in order to produce courtyards, variety, and a more open configuration. Each unit includes three different elevations and finished space of 1,820 (two story with loft) in the non-garage units, 2,440 (three story) in the interior single-car garage units, and 2,770 (three story) in the end two-care garage unit.

The Company has also built custom homes on speculation or under contract with owners. Current plan inventory for custom homes includes eight house types, each with two elevations that range in square footage from 4,000 sq. ft. to 8,000 sq. ft. In the future, the Company will modify these plans to accommodate its clients, or it will develop new plans on a fee basis under a design-build contract. Although the Company has temporarily suspended its activity in custom homes in favor of production housing, it expects to reenter this market at sometime in the future. In all cases where the Company develops the plans, it will retain ownership of the designs, but restricts its ability to build such plans more than once in any community.

Product Under Development

The Manchester Series is a small-lot program offering six models ranging in size from 3,200 sq. ft. to 5,200 sq. ft. that offer a number of structural options designed to expand the base house and create variety in exterior design. Each model in this series includes three elevations with options that include porches, rear sunrooms, lofts, stacked bays, and three-car garages.

LOT INVENTORIES

Current lot inventories, including rolling options on finished lots, total more than 930 and new land positions are being evaluated almost daily. In addition to finished lots in two locations, the Company has just completed the feasibility studies on three additional sites that it expects to develop for its own use.

SPECULATIVE CONSTRUCTION

LOT INVENTORIES AND FUTURE PROJECTS

	2002	2003	2004	2005	2006
Current Projects Under Const					
Potomac Commons (singles)	24	30	36	42	48
Baywood Station (towns)	36	40	48	54	54
Fairfax Park (singles)	15	30	36	42	48
Projects in Planning					
Stonehenge (towns)	10	24	36	40	48
Grubby Thicket (singles)				10	30
The Reserve (singles)				10	30
Unidentified Projects					
Project 1 (towns)				24	48
Project 2 (singles)				24	36
Project 3 (towns)				24	36
Total	85	124	156	270	378

The Company is very cautious when it comes to speculative construction. A formal written request must be initiated by a staff member and then authorized by each department head and the president, in order to initiate such construction. Speculative construction establishes certain additional risks to the Company and it will therefore be limited. While it is the intention of the Company to limit such risks, it will accept them in those cases where they are perceived to be minimal and the Company would benefit from a more even production pace while satisfying a market demand.

CUSTOMER CARE

The ABC Building Company is committed to a customer focus and will do everything within reason to protect the goodwill of its clients, purchasers, and homeowners, and to insure customer satisfaction and a high rate of referrals. All employees are routinely expected to communicate directly with its clients, purchasers, and homeowners, and its processes are designed to initiate an exchange of information that will both inform and support its customers. The Company expects to maintain a reputation for pro-active customer care.

Post-settlement warranty service is centralized and maintained by a professional staff outside of the responsibilities for construction management. The warranty service process is highly defined and documented. Every effort has been made to provide an easy method for the homeowner to initiate a service request, (by phone, fax, or the Internet), and response-time is a key focus of all post-settlement service staff.

THE MARKETING PLAN

THE MARKET AND OPPORTUNITY TARGET

The Company commissions a broad market report annually in order to better understand current market conditions and potential opportunities for the Company (see study attached). In addition, the company requires an individual market study during the feasibility study period for all proposed projects.

The Company is currently active in three distinct market segments: (1) upscale semi-custom single-family detached markets in both Montgomery County in Maryland and Fairfax County in Virginia, (2) mass market single-family detached markets in Fairfax and Loudoun Counties in Virginia and Montgomery and Howard Counties in Maryland, and (3) mass market single-family attached (townhouse) markets in Montgomery County in Maryland and Loudoun County in Virginia. Studies indicate the following with regard to these markets:

Upscale Semi-Custom Single-Family Detached

The average sales price for this category over the past two-years has been $514,000 including options and extras. Sixty-seven percent of buyers in this product line are between the ages of forty-one and fifty-nine, with a median household income of $134,500.

Mass Market Single-Family Detached

The average sales price for this category over the past two-year has been $467,000 including options and extras. Seventy-one percent of the buyers in this product line are between the ages of thirty-three and fifty-two, with a median household income of $97,200.

Mass Market Single-Family Attached

The average sales price for this category over the past two-years has been $302,000 including options and extras. Seventy-four percent of the buyers in this product line are between the ages of twenty-eight and thirty-seven, with a median household income of $87,400.

A SURVEY OF COMPETITION

A survey of competition is required by the Company during the feasibility study period for each new project and also for the broad market study conducted annually by its sales and marketing consultant (see broad market study attached).

SALES AND PRODUCTION TARGETS FIVE-YEAR PLANNING PERIOD THE ABC BUILDING COMPANY, INC. AND AFFILIATES					
	2002	2003	2004	2005	2006
Sales	95	155	220	330	400
Starts	110	150	225	365	460
Closings	85	134	186	296	348

Note: Projections for 2005 and 2006 are based on loose approximations; not all of the land required has been identified.

THE SALES AND MARKETING CONSULTANT

The ABC Building Company, Inc. has entered into a two-year contract with CentraMo Marketing for sales and marketing consulting services that include new product development, participation in focus groups, an annual broad market report, individual marketing feasibility studies, and other requirements as may be required.

OPERATIONS

The operations of the ABC Building Company include a series of policies, procedures, and processes that have resulted from a broad range of strategies.

STRATEGIES

This plan reflects a number of strategies developed by the Company in order to insure its growth and development. Some such strategies include the following:

Land Acquisition and Development Strategies

The Company expects to continue purchasing finished lots in large planned unit developments as it begins to purchase raw ground for future development. The initial strategy of the Company was to establish itself quickly through the purchase of finished lots under rolling option contracts. Although competition is more intense under these conditions, the Company has established its ability to compete successfully against other home builders in this market.

The second stage of development in this area is underway. The Company will continue to identify parcels of ground that represent opportunities for future development and home building. Every effort will be made to purchase such ground on phase takedowns, with seller take-back financing in order to conserve cash. At the current time, the Company is limiting its activity to A and B locations in Montgomery County in Maryland and both Fairfax and Loudoun counties in Virginia. The Company expects to expand its activity to include some C locations in both Howard and Frederick Counties in Maryland beginning in 2003 or 2004.

Market Strategies

The Company expects to remain flexible with regard to its product line. It will develop both mass-market and upscale single family detached and attached product. Designs will feature exceptional exterior and interior detail. Market strategies for each new project will be driven by both an internal market study developed by staff and a market study commissioned by a local marketing consultant. Surveys and focus groups will be used to validate the product, as well as the sales and marketing program.

In general, product lines will include slightly more in standard features than the current builders offer. The Company recognizes the need to create perceived value in the minds of its potential purchasers. During feasibility periods on new projects, the Company will define the market target, establish the buyer profile, set market share targets, and identify absorption rates.

In addition to site-specific advertising and sales promotion, the Company will establish an ongoing public relations program, participate in the local home builder's association, and seek recognition for both its products and its management practice.

Product Development Strategies

The Company will evaluate product strategies for each new building project before fully engaging an architect. A team that includes senior staff, representatives of the front-line sales and production team, a marketing consultant, and an architect, will develop new products. The Company will use several architects to help develop its product lines in order to insure variety. The first step in the product development process will be to identify some substantial and sustainable competitive advantage that can be developed, and then be included in its product mix, designs, specifications, scopes of work, and option strategies. The Company will use architectural, engineering, and management skills to design and refine products, and then it will encourage the participation of other staff members and use focus groups in order to validate those designs.

Pricing Strategies

Cost-based pricing formulas create opportunities for both under-pricing and over-pricing and will not be used except in those cases where the Company is submitting a competitive bid on a one-of-kind custom home. In order to insure proper pricing, the Company first establishes what the market will pay for the home that it intends to build. Each new project will begin with a market study that includes a competitive analysis. Based on these facts, the Company can then convert those facts to an architectural design and specifications that will satisfy the anticipated market target and capture the market share that is anticipated. This approach will help determine the velocity that is likely and permit the Company to mobilize a production capacity to meet the anticipated demand. By working backward from the market price and protecting margin, the Company can determine what it can afford to pay for ground. This is an exercise that will be performed during the feasibility analysis on every new project.

Cost Reduction Strategies

The Company will develop and implement cost reduction initiatives on a continuing basis. As initiatives are fully implemented, new initiatives will be developed and initiated.

Human Resource Strategies

The Company will maintain a process designed to recruit, develop, manage, and train a departmentalized team. Management understands that the future success of the Company will depend largely on its staff. An employee orientation manual is currently under development and the Company expects to have it completed by the end of the year.

Each new employee will receive a formal orientation by both the hiring administrator and the President of the Company. The administrative orientation will be focus on company policies and procedures, and the orientation with the President will focus on culture, processes, and management practice. The Company recognizes the importance of its employees and will make every effort to inform them and enable them to take a very active role in every phase of operations.

E-Business Strategies

Recognizing the importance of information management and collaboration, the Company will establish an e-business strategy and update it annually. These are strategies that currently focus largely on the development of an integrated, web-based information management system based on current technologies, that will improve revenue opportunities and decrease operational inefficiencies for the Company. The Company is currently working on the development of its website, implementing improved email technology, high-speed internet access, a formal security protocol, the improvement of its cellular phone network, and improvements to its back office and accounting business systems. The Company expects to use the Internet as a solution for improving its collaboration and information sharing.

Management Strategies

The Company currently amends and updates written policy directives, portions of the business plan, an organization chart, a safety plan, and a training manual (under development) that are maintained in data files on its server and available to every employee. The Company recognizes the ongoing need to create operating efficiencies by clearly defining policies and procedures, improving back office systems, better defining processes, improving communications, developing a partnership program with trade contractors and suppliers, improving the bidding and contracting process through the use of written specifications and scopes of work, increasing production quality through the use of checklists and homeowner involvement, and maintaining a streamlined process for special option requests.

The Company is also in the process of developing a strategic partnership with a title company in order to establish a participation in title fees, and reducing the cost of funds through credit line financing and additional investment.

Customer Care and Public Relations Strategies

The Company is committed to a level of pro-active customer care that will insure customer satisfaction, provide referral sales, and increase the standing of the Company in the community. The Company maintains a public relations program at the corporate level that is designed to support the activities within the various operating entities.

POLICY

Policy for the ABC Building Company is maintained in a number of written directives that are initiated by senior staff and approved by the president. A complete copy of corporate policy is maintained in a public file on the server for the benefit of staff and staff members are encouraged to submit suggestions that would modify policy (see policy statements attached).

FEASIBILITY STUDIES

Prior to the purchase of any land, a complete feasibility study must be made by staff and presented to the directors of the Company. In additional to a complete financial package including a pro-forma income statement, a life of project summary, a cash budget, a loan summary, and other related schedules and worksheets, each project feasibility study must include the following:

◆ A phase I environmental study

◆ A soils study including soil borings and/or a seismic survey

◆ Photographs of the site

◆ A market study with a competitive survey

◆ Departmental summaries from Sales, Production, Land, and Finance.

◆ Product specifications and scopes of work

PRODUCT DEVELOPMENT

The ABC Building Company creates new product using a design team concept. The team includes the architect, a marketing consultant, the president, and both sales and production employees as well as the department heads. The Company will attempt to validate designs using focus groups and encourage the participation of other staff members in order to insure the success of the product.

A QUALITY BUILDING PROCESS

It is the Company's belief that a quality building program generally consists of seven major requirements: (1) a well-qualified staff, (2) uniform contracts, specifications and scopes of work, (3) the involvement of engineers, (4) the involvement of customers, (5) required frame and floor checks, (6) a quality assurance program, and (7) oversight inspections.

Well-Qualified Staff—The Company believes that its Project Managers are a key to the success of their construction program. They must be well qualified with a background that demonstrates both skill and knowledge.
Uniform Contracts, Specifications, and Scopes of Work—The Company will initiate

uniform labor and material contracts, project specifications, and scopes of work for all new projects.

The Involvement of Engineers—The Company uses soils engineers for all footing inspections and structural engineers are employed during the product development process and to make field inspections where required.

Customer Involvement—The Company encourages customer involvement during the construction process. In addition to site inspections that may be scheduled by the purchaser, each purchaser is expected meet with the construction manager or his representative on at least three occasions during the construction process including, (1) a pre-construction meeting, (2) a pre-drywall walk, and (3) an orientation.

Required Frame and Floor Checks—The Company requires on-site field construction managers to conduct frame and floor checks.

Oversight Inspections—The Company recognizes that oversight is critical for quality in construction. On-site construction managers are required to walk their houses every day and area construction supervisors must validate both the process and the standards of quality

MANAGEMENT AND THE MANAGEMENT STRUCTURE

The management and management structure of the ABC Building Company is based on the belief that the Company is only as strong as its employees and the environment within which they work. In order for employees to provide the support necessary, they must be knowledgeable and empowered to participate. Both the organization and culture is critical to the success of the Company.

THEORY, PRINCIPLES AND PRACTICES

The Company is grounded in the belief that extraordinary management begins with a business plan that includes both strategies and financial plans that are driven by facts. Policies, procedures, and processes must be clearly defined and each employee is expected to work within those policies, procedures, and processes.

ORGANIZATION CHART

The attached organizational chart reflects a horizontal network with soft vertical alignment. The Company encourages the active participation of its employees in management activities; it believes in communication, empowering its employees, and encouraging the participation of its employees in the management process. The company is currently building staff and developing the requirements for high-production home building. The Company has experienced a very high level of growth, which was targeted by management from the beginning. The following is the current organization chart and includes both existing personnel as well as those new positions that have been identified for the future:

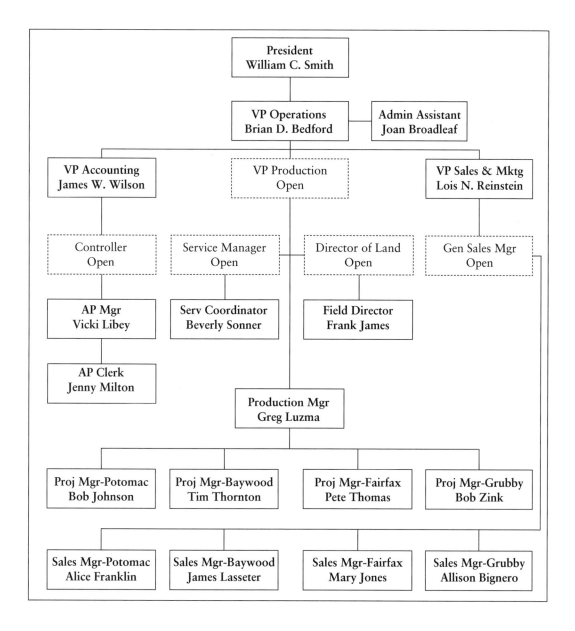

BIOGRAPHIES

OWNERS

William C. Smith

Mr. Smith graduated from The American University in Washington, D.C. in 1979, with a Bachelors Degree in Business Administration. Following his graduation from college, Mr. Smith owned his own home building company for five years and held various senior management positions with other local home building companies, until he formed the ABC Building Company in 2000. He has more than twenty years of home building experience and he has an established reputation for quality construction, proactive customer care, and the ability to produce positive financial results.

Robert D. Jones

Mr. Jones is a successful local land developer with more than thirty years of experience in both residential and commercial land and development. Throughout his career, he has developed a number of benchmark communities that include Rivers Edge, Columbia Commons, Ballston Reserve, Pencley, Stone Ridge Preserve, Fort Hunt Station, Potomac Commons, Baywood, and Fairfax Park.

John P. Doe

Mr. Doe is a relative of the President and an investor in the Company who is now fully retired after a considerable career in corporate law.

Senior Managers

Brian D. Bedford, Vice President of Operations

Mr. Bedford is a graduate of Northwestern University in Chicago, Illinois with a Bachelors Degree in Business Administration. In addition to owning and operating his own home building company for more that twelve years, he has also worked in senior positions for two large local production home builders. He has a reputation for quality construction, proactive customer care, and unusually strong leadership skills.

Lois N. Reinstein, Vice President of Sales and Marketing

Ms. Reinstein is a graduate of the University of Maryland with a Bachelors Degree in Consumer Economics. In addition to her experience as a Sales Manager, a General Sales manager and the Director of Marketing for a large local home building company, she has also received awards from the Sales and Marketing Committee of the Suburban Maryland Building Industry Association for outstanding sales volume in 1995 and 1996 and General Sales Manager of the Year in 1998. She holds a Brokers License in both the states of Maryland and Virginia and she remains an active participant with the local home builder's associations.

James W. Wilson, Vice President of Accounting and Finance

Mr. Wilson is a graduate of George Washington University in Washington D.C., where he received a Bachelors Degree in Accounting and Finance. He is a Certified Public Accountant and currently holds the position of Chairman of the Business and Finance Committee of the Northern Virginia Building Industry Association. In addition to his work as a senior auditor for a top-ten accounting firm, he has also worked in the housing industry for more than fourteen years.

Advisors

Frederick C. Backus, CPA

Mr. Backus is the President and COO of Backus and Associates, P.A., his own accounting firm. He has more than thirty years experience in private accounting practice and has written a book on accounting and finance for home builders.

David H. Dryer, President, XYZ Corporation

Mr. Dryer is currently President of the XYZ Corporation where he has worked for more than ten years in senor positions. XYZ is a local civil engineering company specializing in residential land planning and site development. Mr. Dryer is a recognized expert in land planning with more than twenty-five years experience.

Robert D. Jones, President and COO, Bayside Development Corporation, Inc.
   See biography above.

Robert B. Miller, President, QRS Ventures, LLC
   Mr. Miller is the sole owner and President of QRS Ventures, LLC, a small, venture capital firm, specializing in expansion-stage financing for growing companies, with offices in both Washington, D.C. and Los Angeles, California. This start-up company has provided financing for more than seven home building companies over the past six years and Mr. Miller is a recognized expert in equity financing for both home builders and land developers.

SALARY SCHEDULES

The following salary schedule reflects the current pay status for those who are currently employed by the Company and the anticipated base salary for others who have been identified for future employment. The base salary for the President has been established to reflect the conservative belief that over-funding base salaries can only lead to an unreasonable burden for the company.

MANAGEMENT COMPENSATION
FIVE-YEAR PHASING PLAN

	Base Salary	2002	2003	2004	2005	2006
President	$150,000					
Vice President, Operations	130,000					
Vice President, Sales & Marketing	125,000	X				
Vice President, Accounting & Finance	110,000	X				
Vice President, Production	110,000		X			
Director of Land & Development	100,000		X			
Warranty Service Manager	75,000			X		
General Sales Manager	90,000				X	
Controller	85,000				X	

Note: Base salaries are at current dollars and do not include profit participation for senior staff (vice presidents) or bonus incentives for middle managers.

COMPENSATION

The Company maintains a compensation program that provides for a competitive base salary and either a discretionary bonus, a bonus resulting from measured results (e.g. a production bonus), or a bonus based on the profitability of the company.

CAPITALIZATION

The ABC Building Company has been capitalized through the sale of stock and its various entities have been capitalized through both personal and corporate investment.

ENTITIES

The ABC Building Company is a standard C Corporation, but it uses separate entities for the construction of new projects. To date, these entities have consisted of LLCs and Limited Liability Companies.

INVESTMENT

From the beginning, investors have played an important part in the equity financing of the ABC Building Company and its related entities. In addition to the sophisticated investors who have purchased stock in the Company, the Company has been successful in its efforts to attract investors for all five of its current projects. These projects were undertaken with investors as follows:

Potomac Commons, LLC
    Potomac Commons, LLC was formed early in 2000 for the specific purpose of building two hundred and fifty single-family detached units in the Potomac Commons Community. It is a project undertaken by the three principle stockholders of the ABC Building Corporation and two principle stockholders of IJK Plumbing Corporation, a large, local residential plumbing contractor. The original short-term investment of $1 million was repaid to the investors, together with interest, in 2001; the company retains the right to draw additional funds as needed, but in no event to exceed the original $1 million.

Baywood Limited Partnership
    The Baywood Limited Partnership was formed in 2000 for the specific purpose of building three hundred townhouses in the Baywood Station Community. The partnership consists of the ABC Building Corporation as general partner, and twelve private investors who each invested $100,000. Although there is an equity draw provision in the agreement, all of the original $1.2 million invested capital was returned to the investors in 2001.

Fairfax Park, LLC
    The Fairfax Park LLC, was formed late in 2000 for the specific purpose of developing the ground and building one hundred and seventy single-family detached homes in the Fairfax Park Community. This is a project undertaken by the three principle stockholders of the ABC Building Company together with four individual investors. Each investor has committed to provide as much as $300,000 in investment as needed, for a total potential investment of $1.3 million. The Company drew down $1.2 million of the total 1.3 million and paid $400,000 back, together with interest, in 2001. It expects to draw down another $500,000 in 2002 and return it together with interest by the end of the year. The Company expects the balance of $800,000 to be returned to the investors, together with interest, sometime in 2003.

Stonehenge Limited Partnership

The Stonehenge Limited Partnership was formed in 2001 for the specific purpose of developing the ground and building one hundred and seventy units in the Stonehenge Community. The partnership consists of the ABC Building Company, as the general partner, and twelve individual, but sophisticated investors, who have invested a total of $1.3 million. The Company expects to return the investment, together with interest over the next three years.

Grubby Thicket, LLC

The Grubby Thicket LLC was formed in early 2002 for the specific purpose of developing the ground and building forty single-family detached units in the Grubby Thicket Subdivision. This is a project undertaken by the three principle stockholders of the ABC Building Company and a single, sophisticated investor. The investor has provided $850,000 in invested capitol, which will be repaid at the rate of $41,250, together with interest, as each home is closed.

FINANCIAL PROJECTIONS

Financial projections for the ABC Building Company and its related companies generally consist of pro-forma income and expense statements, life of project projections, and cash budgets, all of which have been provided as exhibits.

> The information presented in these financial plans has been developed for management purposes only. They have not been audited and the Company therefore makes no representations regarding their accuracy.

PRO-FORMA INCOME AND EXPENSE STATEMENTS

Pro-forma financial statements are prepared for each project in conjunction with the initial financial feasibility studies.

LIFE OF PROJECT PROJECTIONS

The Company prepares a Life of Project Projection for each new project during the feasibility period. These forecasts result from worksheets that are provided by each department and then consolidated for presentation. They are adjusted annually based on actual experience and changes that can be reasonably anticipated as the project moves toward completion.

CASH BUDGET

The Company prepares cash budgets for each project with a consolidated summary on a regular basis. Actual figures are reviewed formally at the end of the second quarter and both cash budgets and the overall business plan are adjusted as part of a mid-year reforecast.

CAPITAL SPENDING

Wherever possible, the Company will plan for significant capital expenditures two or more years in advance. The Company recognizes the importance of maintaining significant cash reserves and will approach capital spending with extreme caution. In general, the company will invest surplus cash in a sweep account and/or short-term bonds.

AUDITING

In addition to audits of financial statements, which will be performed as needed from time-to-time, the company will conduct an internal operation audit every other year beginning in 2003. Such informal audits will be conducted by a third-party representative, selected by the board of directors, for the purpose of verifying company-wide compliance with policy, procedures, and processes.

THE FUTURE

The staff and management of the ABC Building Company are dedicated to a long-term goal of growth through the acquisition of other similar companies operating in other similar markets. They will develop the company with the potential to either acquire other home building companies or to become acquired by a national builder. The critical requirements for the sale of a company include the development of well-conceived business plans, written policies, standardized procedures, the development of effective processes, a high level of customer satisfaction, a reputation for effective management, and a substantial earnings history. These are the same requirements for a successful homebuilding company. Whether the Company is ever sold is immaterial, it will always remain an option for the owner or owners.

CONFIDENTIALITY AGREEMENT

RECITALS:

The ABC Building Company, Inc., its officers and other unnamed individuals, (hereinafter referred to as the "Company") have developed a strategic and financial plan for the ABC Building Company (hereinafter referred to as the "Business Plan"). Having completed the Business Plan, the Company must now secure equity and debt capital, as well as negotiate leases and/or purchase real property. In the course of such transactions, detailed information regarding the Business Plan must be disclosed to various individuals, companies, and corporations (hereinafter referred to as "Prospect(s)"). It is extremely important to the Company that all information regarding or related to the Business Plan be held in the strictest confidence of the Prospect(s) and it is the intention of this document to protect that confidentiality.

For and in consideration of the sum of one dollar ($1.00) as well as the mutual promises

made in this Confidentiality Agreement between_____

_____, the Prospect(s) and the Com-

pany, as set forth above, the parties hereby agree as follows:

1. All information contained in a certain business plan entitled "A Strategic and Financial Plan for the Next Five Years," together with the attachments, shall be held in the strictest confidence by the Prospect(s) and, except as it becomes necessary to direct the efforts of others working directly for the Prospect(s), no disclosure will be made to any individual, company, or corporate representative of any information contained therein, without the express written consent of the Company.

2. The Prospect(s) understands the sensitive nature of the information contained in the Business Plan, the potential for damages to the Company should this information be disclosed without their consent, and hereby accepts the responsibility to keep it secret and confidential.

In the event that any provision of this agreement is determined to be invalid and or unenforceable by a final decision of a court of competent jurisdiction, it shall not affect the remainder of the agreement, which shall survive and remain in full force and effect.

The Prospect(s) especially warrants or represents that he, she, or they has the ability to enter into this agreement and perform all obligations hereunder, and that there are no restrictions or obligations to third parties, which would in any way detract from or affect the performance of obligations set forth herein.

Any dispute that arises hereunder shall be resolved by binding arbitration pursuant to the rules of the American Arbitration Association or the rules of arbitration recommended by the State of Maryland.

In the event that any arbitration or litigation is required to enforce any of the provisions of this agreement, the prevailing party of said litigation shall be entitled to recover from the other party, all costs thereof including reasonable attorneys' fees.

This agreement shall be governed by and interpreted in accordance with the laws of the State of Maryland.

EXECUTED this _____ day of, 2002, in Montgomery County, in the State of Maryland.

Prospect: _____

Prospect: _____

ABC Building Company, Inc.

By: _____
                   President

APPENDIX B

A SAMPLE FINANCING PROPOSAL

Appendix B has been included to demonstrate the essential documents that should accompany any request for construction financing. For the purposes of illustration and to keep the contents of this book brief, not all of the documents referred to in the table of contents have been included. Such documents are unique to the property; others are typically provided by consultants or other professionals, and still others will vary considerably based on the location of the home building company. Those documents that have been included will serve as examples and help the reader understand the essential character of the loan submission.

ABC Building Company, Inc.
1234 Anyplace Drive, Suite 300
Rockville, MD 20850

June 12, 2002

Mr. Kevin Washington
Best Bank U S A
789 Commerce Court
Potomac, Maryland

Dear Kevin:

In accordance with our conversation, please find enclosed the formal loan request that we discussed yesterday. We are excited about the potential for this unique property and believe that it represents a unique opportunity for the ABC Building Company. Grubby Thicket is well located and the market remains very strong for mass-market single-family detached homes in this price range. As I indicated, we will be developing this property and building in a Limited Liability Company (LLC) with Mr. Jason D. Peterson, President of Peterson Enterprises, Inc. I have known Jason for a number of years and look forward to the possibility of using this project as a springboard to build a long-term business relationship with him. I have enclosed a copy of our proposed documents for Grubby Thicket LLC for your review. We expect to close our deal next week and I will forward copies of the executed documents at that time. Any commitment from your bank would, of course, be contingent upon the satisfactory execution of these documents with equity funding at the time of closing. The closing of the property will coincide with the closing of the loan.

We have completed our internal feasibility study. In addition to the financial plans for the project, current financial statements for the ABC Building Company, Inc., and a personal financial statement, I am also providing a number of additional documents for your review (see the Table of Contents). If you will give me a call after you have had a chance to review these documents, I will schedule a lunch with you and we can discuss the conditions of the deal further.

Please note that I am on a short fuse. The site plan was just approved and we expect to settle in the next ninety (90) days. Anything you can do to expedite the loan process would be appreciated.

Respectfully,

William C. Smith
President

THE GRUBBY THICKET PROPOSAL
FORTY (40) SINGLE FAMILY DETACHED HOMES
MONTGOMERY COUNTY, MARYLAND

THE ABC BUILDING COMPANY, INC.

Loan   Amount (revolver) $7,216,000

Requested: Rate   1% floating over Prime

                      Term   30 months with one optional 6 month extension

                      Disbursements
                          Land Advance $ 936,000
                          Land Development $1,640,000
                          Construction $4,640,000

                      Fee 1% of $72,160,000 to be paid $36,080 at settlement and $36,080 to be paid from first construction draws as they are disbursed.

Borrower: Grubby Thicket, LLC

                      Loan Analysis: *Valuation $14,820,000
                                           Loan Requested (revolver) $ 7,216,000
                                           Loan Ratio (maximum per unit)   80%
                                           Maximum Loan Per Unit $ 296,400

                      Guarantor: ABC Building Company, Inc.
                                           William and Buffy Smith

                      * Valuation is based upon the projected gross sales of forty (40) units with an average sales price of $370,500, exclusive of anticipated income from the sale of options and lot premiums, as established by budgets and income projections.

APPENDIX C

NAHB CHART OF ACCOUNTS

1000–1990   **Assets**
1000–1090   **Cash**
1010   Petty cash
1020   Cash on deposit, general
1030   Cash on deposit, payroll
1040   Cash on deposit, savings and money market
1050   Cash on deposit, held in escrow
1100–1190   **Short-Term Investments**
1110   Certificates of Deposit
1120   Marketable Securities
1130   Government Securities
1190   Other Short-term Investments
1200–1290   **Receivables**
1210   Accounts receivable, trade
1220   Accounts receivable, other
1230   Notes receivable
1250   Mortgage notes receivable, current year
1260   Due on construction and development loans
1270   Accrued interest receivable
1280   Allowance for doubtful accounts
1290   Retentions (retainage) receivable
1300–1390   **Inventories**
1310   Construction materials inventory
1320   Land held for development
1330   Property held for Remodeling
1400–1490   **Construction Work in Progress**
1410   Land and land development
1412   Accumulated allocations, land and land development costs
1420   Developed lots
1430   Direct construction cost
1440   Indirect construction cost
1470   Cost in excess of billings
1500–1590   **Finished Units and Other Inventory**

1510   Finished units
1520   Model homes
1530   Trade-ins and repossessions
1600–1690   Other Current Assets
1610   Refundable deposits
1620   Prepaid expenses
1630   Employee advances
1650   Due from affiliated companies or subsidiaries
1660   Due from officers, stockholders, owners or partners
1670   Deposits on plans
1690   Other current assets
1700–1790   Investments and Other Assets
1710   Investments, long-term
1720   Cash surrender value of officers' life insurance
1730   Investments in affiliated entities
1750   Mortgage notes receivable, long-term
1760   Due from affiliated companies or subsidiaries, long-term
1770   Due from officers, owners, stockholders, long-term
1780   Organization cost
1800–1890   Property, Plant, and Equipment
1810   Land
1820   Buildings
1825   Rental Property
1827   Recreation amenities
1830   Office furniture and equipment
1840   Vehicles
1850   Construction equipment
1870   Model home furnishings
1880   Leasehold improvements
1890   Computer equipment and software
1900–1990   Accumulated Depreciation
1920   Accumulated depreciation, buildings
1925   Accumulated depreciation, rental properties
1927   Accumulated depreciation, recreation amenities
1930   Accumulated depreciation, office furniture and equipment
1940   Accumulated depreciation, vehicles
1950   Accumulated depreciation, construction equipment
1970   Accumulated depreciation, model home furnishings
1980   Accumulated depreciation, leasehold improvements
1990   Accumulated depreciation, computer equipment and software
2000–2990   Liabilities and Owners' Equity
2000–2090   Deposits by Customers
2010   Contract deposits
2030   Tenant security deposit
2040   Advance rent collected
2100–2190   Accounts Payable

2110	Accounts payable, trade
2120	Retentions payable
2190	Accounts payable, other

2200–2290   Notes Payable

2200	Line of credit payable
2220	Acquisitions and development loans payable (old 252 in prior accounts)
2230	Construction loans payable
2240	Current portion of long-term debt
2290	Notes payable, other

2300–2490   Other Current Liabilities

2310	Social Security and Medicare
2320	Federal payroll tax withheld and accrued
2330	State payroll tax withheld and accrued
2340	Other payroll withholdings
2345	Union withholding and benefits Payable
2350	Sales and use taxes payable
2360	Real estate taxes payable
2370	Income taxes payable
2390	Accrued interest payable
2400	Accrued salaries and wages payable
2410	Accrued commissions payable
2411	Accrued pension and profit-sharing expenses
2420	Workers' compensation insurance payable
2425	Other accrued expenses
2430	Deferred income
2440	Due to affiliated companies or subsidiaries
2450	Due to officers, stockholders, owners, and partners
2480	Billings in excess of costs
2490	Other current liabilities

2500–2890   Long-Term Liabilities

2510	Long-term Notes Payable
2530	Mortgage notes payable
2600	Deferred income tax payable
2610	Due to affiliated companies or subsidiaries, long-term
2620	Due to officers, stockholders, owners, long-term, and partners
2700	Other long-term liabilities

2900–2990   Owners' Equity

2900	Common stock
2910	Additional paid in capital
2920	Retained earnings
2930	Treasury Stock
2940	Unrealized holding gain
2950	Partnership or proprietorship account
2960	Distributions, dividends, and draws

3000–3990   Sales, Revenues, and Cost of Sales

3000–3490   Sales and Revenues

3000   Sales, land held for development
3050   Sales, developed lots
3100   Sales, single-family speculative
3110   Sales, single-family production
3120   Sales, single-family custom designed
3125   Sales, single family custom, no land
3130   Sales, residential remodeling
3133   Sales, commercial and industrial remodeling
3135   Sales, insurance restoration
3137   Sales, repairs
3140   Sales, multifamily
3150   Sales, commercial and industrial
3160   Sales, trade-ins, and repossessions
3190   Sales, other
3200   Rental property income
3210   Common area reimbursements
3220   Other reimbursements
3230   Parking fee income
3240   Amenities and facilities income
3360   Construction management fee income
3370   Design Fees Collected
3400   Miscellaneous income
3410   Interest income
3420   Dividend income
3450   Earned discounts
3490   Sales concessions and discounts
3500–3790   Cost of Sales
3500   Cost of sales, land held for development
3550   Cost of sales, developed lots
3600   Cost of sales, single-family speculative
3610   Cost of sales, single-family production
3620   Cost of sales, single-family custom designed
3625   Cost of sales, single family custom, no land
3630   Cost of sales, remodeling
3633   Cost of sales, commercial and industrial remodeling
3635   Cost of sales, insurance restoration
3637   Cost of sales, repairs
3640   Cost of sales, multifamily
3650   Cost of sales, commercial and industrial
3660   Cost of sales, trade-ins
3690   Cost of sales, other
3700   Direct construction cost for prior periods
3800–3899   Costs of Construction—Remodeling
3810   Direct Labor
3820   Labor Burden
3830   Building Material

3840   Subcontractors
3850   Rental Equipment
3860   Other Direct Construction Costs
3870   Professional Design Fees
4000–4990   Indirect Construction Cost
4000–4090   Salaries and Wages
4010   Superintendents
4020   Laborers
4030   Production manager
4040   Architects, drafters, estimators, and purchasers
4050   Other indirect construction wages
4100–4190   Payroll Taxes and Benefits
4110   Payroll taxes
4120   Workers' compensation insurance
4130   Health and accident insurance
4140   Retirement, pension, and profit sharing
4150   Union benefits
4190   Other benefits
4200–4290   Field Office Expenses
4210   Rent, field office
4230   Repairs and maintenance, field office
4250   Utilities, field office
4260   Telephone, field office
4265   Mobile phones, pagers, and radios
4290   Other field office expenses
4300–4390   Field Warehouse and Storage Expenses
4310   Rent, field warehouse and storage
4330   Repairs and maintenance, field warehouse and storage
4350   Utilities, field warehouse and storage
4360   Telephone, field warehouse and storage
4400–4490   Construction Vehicles, Travel, and Entertainment
4410   Lease payments, construction vehicles
4420   Mileage reimbursement
4430   Repairs and maintenance, construction vehicles
4440   Operating expenses, construction vehicles
4450   Taxes, licenses, and insurance, construction vehicles
4460   Travel, construction department
4470   Customer business entertainment, construction
4480   Training and education, construction
4490   Recruiting Fees and Expenses, Construction
4500–4590   Construction Equipment
4510   Rent, construction equipment
4530   Repairs and maintenance, construction equipment
4540   Operating expenses, construction equipment
4550   Taxes and insurance, construction equipment
4560   Small tools and supplies

4600–4690   Expenses for Maintaining Unsold Units and Units Under Construction
4610   Temporary utilities
4620   Trash maintenance
4640   Lawn care
4650   Utilities, completed units
4660   Repairs and maintenance, completed units
4700–4790   Warranty and Customer Service
4710   Salaries and wages, warranty
4720   Material, warranty
4730   Subcontractor, warranty
4790   Other, warranty expenses
4800–4890   Depreciation Expenses
4820   Depreciation, construction office
4830   Depreciation, warehouse
4840   Depreciation, construction vehicles
4850   Depreciation, construction equipment
4900–4990   Other
4910   Insurance and bonding expenses
4920   Builders risk insurance
4990   Absorbed indirect costs
5000–5990   Financing Expenses
5000–5090   Interest
5010   Interest on line of credit
5020   Interest on notes payable
5030   Interest expense on developed lots
5040   Interest incurred on construction loans
5050   Interest on completed inventory
5090   Interest expense, Other
5100–5190   Construction Loan Points and Fees
5120   Points and fees
5130   Appraisal and related fees
5140   Inspection fees
5200–5290   Closing Costs
5210   Closing costs
5220   Title and recording
5230   Fees, commitment
6000–6990   Sales and Marketing Expenses
6000–6090   Sales Salaries, and Commissions
6010   Sales manager's compensation
6030   Salaries, sales personnel
6040   Sales commissions, in-house
6050   Sales commissions, outside
6090   Other sales office Salaries and Wages
6100–6190   Payroll Taxes and Benefits, Sales and Marketing
6110   Payroll taxes, sales and marketing
6120   Workers' compensation insurance, sales and marketing

6130   Health and accident insurance, sales and marketing
6140   Retirement, pension, and profit-sharing plans, sales and marketing
6190   Other benefits

6200–6290   Sales Office Expenses
6210   Rent, sales office
6230   Repairs and maintenance, sales office
6250   Utilities, sales office
6260   Telephone, sales office
6270   Supplies, sales office

6300–6390   Advertising and Sales Promotion
6310   Print advertising
6320   Radio advertising
6325   Television advertising
6330   Internet fees, web page design and maintenance costs
6340   Brochures and catalogues
6350   Signs
6355   Billboards
6365   Promotions
6370   Agency commissions
6380   Multiple listing fees
6390   Public relations
6395   Referral Fees

6400–6490   Sales Vehicles, Travel, and Entertainment
6410   Lease payments, sales vehicles
6420   Mileage reimbursement
6430   Repairs and maintenance, sales vehicles
6440   Operating expenses, sales vehicles
6450   Taxes, licenses, insurance, sales vehicles
6460   Travel, sales and marketing
6470   Customer business entertainment

6600–6690   Model Home Maintenance
6610   Rent or lease payments, model home furnishings
6620   Model home rent or lease payments
6625   Model home decorating fees
6630   Repairs and maintenance, model homes
6650   Utilities, model homes
6670   Lawn and landscaping care model homes
6680   Cleanup, model homes
6690   Interest on model homes

6700–6790   Sales and Marketing Fees
6710   Market research and consultation
6720   Interior design fee
6770   Recruiting fees and expenses, sales and marketing personnel
6780   Training and education expenses

6800–6890   Depreciation
6810   Depreciation, sales office

6830   Depreciation, sales vehicles
6870   Depreciation, model home furnishings, and decorations

6900–6990   Other Marketing Expenses

6930   Sales concessions
6940   Buydowns
6999   Other sales and marketing expenses

7000–7990   Operating and Management Expenses, Rental Operations

7000–7090   Property Management

7010   Property manager's compensation
7030   Salaries and Wages, property management personnel
7040   Commissions, in-house
7050   Commissions, outside
7060   Salaries and Wages to maintenance personnel
7070   Payroll taxes and benefits, rental operations
7072   Workers' compensation insurance, rental
7073   Health and accident insurance, rental
7074   Retirement, pension, and profit-sharing plans, rental
7079   Other benefits, rental

7100–7190   Rental Expenses

7110   Advertising
7130   Credit reports
7190   Other rental expenses

7200–7290   Administrative Expenses, Rental Operations

7220   Management and service fees
7230   Office expenses
7240   Telephone
7250   Tenant bad debts
7260   Collection costs
7290   Other administrative expenses

7300–7390   Professional Services, Rental Operations

7310   Legal services
7320   Accounting services
7330   Market research
7390   Other professional services, rental operations

7400–7490   Operating Expenses, Rental Operations

7410   Utilities
7420   Engineering
7430   Janitorial
7440   Trash removal service
7450   Exterminating
7460   Snow removal
7470   Other contractual services
7480   Vehicles and equipment, rental operations
7490   Other rental operations expenses

7500–7590   Taxes and Insurance, Rental Operations

7510   Real estate property taxes

7520   Personal property taxes
7530   Franchise taxes
7540   License fees
7560   Workers' compensation insurance
7570   Insurance, rental operations
7590   Other taxes and insurance, rental operations
7690   Maintenance and Repairs, Rental Operations
7610   Tenant redecorating
7630   Maintenance contracts and services
7640   Ground maintenance and repairs
7650   Vehicle maintenance and repairs, rental operations
7660   Equipment maintenance and repairs, rental operations
7670   Amenities maintenance and repairs
7700–7790   Financing Expense, Rental Operations
7710   Interest on mortgage payable
7720   Interest on long-term notes payable
7800–7890   Depreciation Expenses, Rental Operations
7810   Depreciation, building
7820   Depreciation, maintenance equipment
7830   Depreciation, vehicles
7840   Depreciation, furniture and fixtures
7850   Depreciation, amenities
7890   Other Depreciation
7900–7990   Other Management and Operating Expenses
8000–8990   General and Administrative Expense
8000–8090   Salaries and Wages
8010   Salaries, owners
8020   Salaries, officers
8030   Salaries, management
8050   Salaries and wages, office and clerical
8090   Other general and administrative salaries and wages
8100–8190   Payroll Taxes and Benefits
8110   Payroll taxes
8120   Workers' compensation insurance
8130   Health and accident insurance
8140   Retirement, pension, and profit-sharing plans
8190   Other employee benefits
8200–8290   Office Expenses
8210   Rent
8220   Office equipment rental
8230   Repairs and maintenance, administrative office space
8240   Repairs and maintenance, administrative office equipment
8250   Utilities, administrative office
8260   Telephone, administrative office
8270   Office supplies, administrative office
8280   Postage and deliveries

8290   Miscellaneous expenses, administrative office

8300–8390   Computer Expenses

8310   Computer supplies
8320   Leases, computer hardware
8330   Leases, computer software
8350   Repairs and maintenance, computer equipment
8360   Maintenance, computer software

8400–8490   Vehicles, Travel, and Entertainment

8410   Lease, administrative vehicles
8420   Mileage reimbursement
8430   Repairs and maintenance, administration vehicles
8440   Operating expense, administration vehicles
8450   Taxes, licenses, and insurance, administration vehicles
8460   Travel
8470   Customer business expense
8480   Meeting expenses
8490   In-house meeting expenses

8500–8590   Taxes

8510   Sales-and-use taxes
8520   Real estate taxes
8530   Personal property taxes
8540   License fees
8590   Other taxes

8600–8690   Insurance

8610   Hazard insurance/Property insurance
8630   General liability insurance
8690   Other insurance

8700–8790   Professional Services

8710   Accounting services
8720   Legal services
8730   Consulting services
8770   Recruiting and hiring
8790   Other professional expenses

8800–8890   Depreciation Expenses

8810   Depreciation, buildings
8830   Depreciation, vehicles
8840   Depreciation, furniture, and equipment
8860   Amortization of leasehold improvement
8870   Depreciation computer equipment and software
8880   Amortization of organization cost
8890   Depreciation, other

8900–8990   General and Administrative Expense, Other

8900   Bad debts
8910   Contributions
8911   Contributions, Political
8920   Dues and subscriptions

8950   Bank charges
8960   Penalties
8990   Training and education expenses
9000–9990   Other Income and Expenses
9100–9190   Other Income
9100   Income from Partnerships, Joint Ventures, S-Corps, and LLCs
9150   Gain or loss on sale of assets
9190   Other
9200–9290   Other Expenses
9200   Extraordinary Expenses
9300–9390   Provision for Income Taxes
9300   Provision for federal income taxes
9320   Provision for state income taxes
9330   Provision for local income taxes

GLOSSARY

absorption costing—accounting method of allocating costs, which recognizes both direct and indirect costs as inventoriable; both costs related to the production process are considered assets

absorption rate—term used to describe the sales pace or anticipated sales for a particular project, usually expressed as the average number of units sold per month

accounts payable—amounts owed by a business for purchases of labor, material, equipment, or other items that have been received and accepted

accounts receivable—money owed to a business by purchasers, owners, or others for products and services received and accepted

accrual accounting—normal accounting basis for home builders in which revenue is recorded when it is earned and costs and balance sheet account changes are recorded when commitments are made

accrued expense—anticipated cost recorded as an expense before the actual expenditure is made

activity—turns input into an output

ADC loan—single loan used by a builder/developer, that combines disbursements for the acquisition of ground, its development, and the construction of houses.

aging schedule—report classifying unpaid accounts (both payables and receivables) by invoice date, which is usually organized in columns by status including current, 31 to 60 days unpaid, 61to90 days unpaid, andmore than 90 days unpaid

allocation—process of assigning costs and revenues to time periods, activities, and inventory according to the benefits received, responsibilities assumed, usage, or other ratio measure

amortization—spreading or prorating the cost of an asset over a specified period in accordance with generally accepted accounting practice

appraisal—unbiased estimate of the nature, quality, value, or utility of an interest in specific real estate; they can be either an evaluation or a valuation. An evaluation is based on a process of estimating fair-market value, investment value, or insurable value as of a specific date; the sales comparison, cost, and income capitalization approaches are all used to establish the current fair-market value

arm's length transaction—ethical business dealing in which neither the buyer nor the seller is unreasonably influenced by the other

asset—anything that is owned that has monetary value

asset turnover ratio—measure of the efficiency of asset employment, expressed as the ratio of a pertinent parameter, such as revenue to the asset

assignment—binding commitment to share a right or privilege, usually as it relates to income, with another

audit—independent, professional evaluation of the conditions for the benefit of others; such as the financial condition or insurance records of a company

audit trail—result of well organized and detailed accounting entry that permits an internal or external auditor to trace any financial transaction to its originating document

balance sheet—financial statement used to evaluate the condition of a company that lists the assets, liabilities, and equity of a business as of a certain date

bankruptcy—condition resulting from a legal declaration that a company is unable to pay its debts

bond—interest-bearing certificate issued by a corporation that is used to raise capital, that promises to pay the holder a specified sum on a specified date

book value—value of stock based on the current equity of a corporation

budget—itemized summary of probable costs, expenses, income, and profit for a particular construction project or portion thereof. Typical construction budgets may be preliminary, pre-construction, or final budgets; preliminary budgets are those prepared during the feasibility period based on historical costs, pre-construction budgets are those prepared prior to or during the construction process based largely on contracts and known costs, or they may be final budgets prepared in anticipation of sales based on as much actual information as possible

business risk—degree of probability that a company will fail or operate unprofitably due to the uncertainty of income or loss resulting from the product, the production process, the market, or regulatory conditions

capital—amount invested in a business that is equal to equity plus long-term liabilities, or fixed assets plus working capital

capital expenditure—purchase of equipment and the like, that will be accounted for as fixed assets and depreciated over a period of years

capitalization—debt and equity funding necessary for a start-up company or a new project

capitalized lease—accounting term for a lease that has to be shown as a liability on the balance sheet

capitalized value of earnings—net profit after taxes divided by an interest rate appropriate for the degree of risks associated with those earnings

capped guarantee—limited or partial loan guarantee intended to protect the lender from losses up to and including a specific sum of money; the cap on such guarantees are typically limited to that portion of the loan which is not secured by collateral

cash budget—estimate of income and disbursements over a period of time that emphasizes the resulting cash flow

cash dividend coverage ratio—measurement used to determine a corporation's ability to continue to pay dividends at the same rate; cash flow from operations divided by current dividends

cash flow—increase or decrease in cash as a result of a particular transaction, or the net increase or decrease in the operating capital of a business over a particular period of time

cash flow forecasting—financial planning tool that establishes period cash balances (usually monthly) based on projections of income and expenses which are developed based on anticipated sales, construction starts, completions, and settlements

cash flow statement—financial statement that describes the cash flow of a business over a particular period of time; not to be confused with a cash flow forecasting which is used for planning and anticipates income, disbursements, and the resulting cash flow

C corporation—standard or ordinary corporation established under Federal and State laws based on Articles of Incorporation, By-Laws, and Minutes; such corporations minimize personal liability, provide for broad-based ownership, and establish the vehicle necessary for public ownership through the sale of stock

chapter 7 bankruptcy—legal category of bankruptcy that leads to the liquidation of a company

chapter 11 bankruptcy—legal category of bankruptcy that amounts to a reorganization process designed to give a debtor a chance to resume normal operations; many of the companies that file for chapter 11 eventually wind up in a chapter 7 liquidation

chart of accounts—list of numerical accounting categories used to record the transactions of a company.

closely held corporation—small company whose stock is not traded and is held by only a few individuals or other companies; a privately held corporation

closing—formal settlement process required to satisfy the conditions of sale, disburse funds, and record the documents necessary to convey title.

collateral—physical or financial assets or interests in assets, owned or controlled by a borrower, that a lender may require to secure the payment of a debt; in the event of a default, the collateral may be sold and the proceeds used to repay the debt

common stock—certificates of ownership with voting rights that are issued by a corporation to its equity investors

compensating balance—account balance or minimum deposit maintained at a bank as a condition of a bank loan; generally established by a provision of a loan agreement

compilation—accounting term used to describe financial statements that are based on management information without any independent evaluation

conforming loans—permanent loans that do not exceed the current maximum loan amount established by federal regulations for governmental mortgage programs

construction line of credit—revolving loan sometimes used to pay costs related to construction where conventional construction loans are not used; such loans are not secured by specific real estate, but are the subject of a loan agreement with considerable conditions and restrictions related to secondary borrowing and the application of loan proceeds

construction/perm loan—residential real estate loan made directly to a property owner that combines both a construction and a permanent loan; under such loans the lot owner has only one settlement, the funds are disbursed as work progresses, and the construction loan automatically converts to a permanent loan on or before a specific date after the loan is fully funded

contribution margin—measurement of profitability that is expressed as a percentage and equal to revenue minus variable costs, divided by revenue

convertible bond—interest-bearing instrument or certificate, which is used to raise debt capital and can be converted to common stock at a particular price at a specific time

convertible preferred stock—preferred stock that can be converted to common stock at a particular price at a specified time

cost of capital—cost of both debt and equity capital as expressed as an annual percentage rate

creditor—any individual, company, or corporation to whom money or its equivalent is owed

cross default—provision is loan documents that provides that a default on one loan will constitute a default on all loans made to the borrower.

current assets—cash and other assets that are convertible to cash within one year

current liabilities—obligations that must be discharged within one year

current ratio—current assets divided by current liabilities

cycle-time—build-time or total construction time, expressed in work-days, that is required to complete the building process; sometimes referred to as the build time

debenture bond—unsecured bond or borrowing instrument in which holders rely on the creditworthiness of the issuer

debt service—amount of money or interest to be paid in order to keep a debt from being in default

debt service ratio—measurement of cash flow relative to required debt service payments that is equal to the available cash flow divided by interest and principal payment

deferred revenue—liability, representing advance receipts for products or services that are to be provided in the future

deferred taxes—future tax liability resulting from the difference between public and tax accounting

depreciation—gradual reduction in the book value of a fixed asset as a result of normal wear and age

direct cost—labor, material, or equipment cost resulting specifically from the construction of a particular unit; sometimes referred to as the costs of "bricks and mortar" and usually defined by a chart of accounts

disbursement—amount of cash paid out

discounted cash flow—analysis technique that determines and compares the net present value of streams of future cash flows

discount rate—charge for funds borrowed from the Federal Reserve Banks by depository institutions; or the interest rate used to determine present values in discount cash flow analysis

divestiture—sale of part of a company (such as a division or a subsidiary corporation), a facility, or a product line

double entry bookkeeping—accounting process by which every transaction results in two balancing entries; debits and credits

driving force variable—internal or external factor which has the executive attention, is a significant influence, and has a pronounced affect on the enterprise

due diligence—analysis or evaluation of conditions and information relative to a specific event such as the purchase of real property or a corporation, or the pricing of a business or its securities

earn-out—provision or condition generally used in the purchase of a business whereby a portion of the purchase price is dependent on a specific future financial result

EBIT—earnings before interest and taxes

entrepreneur—one who plans, organizes, operates, and assumes the risk of a business venture with the expectation of realizing profit; one who shifts resources from areas of low productivity and yield to areas of higher productivity and yield

equity—difference between fair market value and the debt recorded against an asset or the accounting value placed on the ownership of a business equal to assets minus liabilities; often used interchangeably with book value, net asset value, net worth, or stockholder's equity. Also refers to an ownership share or interest in a business that is typically evidenced by common or preferred stock certificates

escrowed funds—money that has been set aside or put in the custody of a third party for release after the fulfillment of specific conditions; in most cases, such escrows have been established by a clause in a contract or by a separate formal escrow agreement

expense—past, current, or future cost recorded in a period in accordance with generally accepted accounting principles

extraordinary items—accounting items in the profit and loss statement that are both unusual and infrequent

factoring—sale of account receivable with no responsibilities for the risk of collection

feasibility analysis—any routine study or professional evaluation of one or more courses of action or alternatives in order to determine the probability of a successful outcome

fidelity bond—instrument that transfers the risk of a dishonest performance by an employee to a third party

fiduciary responsibility—trust for which one is accountable; a director of a corporation has a fiduciary responsibility to its stockholders

financial analyst—professional who is qualified to study public firms and issue research reports

financial character—those attributes or qualities of a borrower that are largely defined by reputation, credit rating, professional standing, and the quality of a loan request; financial character is carefully considered by both private and institutional lenders and the desire to make a loan is often based more on financial character than it is on a projected return

financial risks—degree of probability or uncertainty that a company will fail to meet its commitments related to fixed obligation debt securities; most business failures stem from or ultimately result in an inability to meet a debt obligation

firm commitment underwriting—public offering in which the underwriter guarantees the sale of the securities offered at a specified price

first position—priority of the lender in the order of repayment in the event that one or more assets are liquidated upon a default by a borrower; also referred to as the primary position or primary debt

fixed asset—asset that has long-term value.

forecast—projection of current trends using existing data. Typical forecasts for home builders include sales, construction starts, and closings for a specific period of time

future value—value of a specific amount of cash on a future date assuming that it will earn a particular interest rate

full disclosure—accounting principle that requires that adequate disclosure be made of anything that would be of interest to an informed investor

gap financing—unsecured financing sometimes used by builders to obtain the funds required over and above a conventional acquisition, development, or construction loan; these funds fill the void between the maximum secured loan amount and the total capital requirement to fund a project

generally accepted accounting principles (GAAP)—rules that govern accounting practice and the preparation of financial statements

gross margin—measure of profitability expressed as a percentage, equal to revenue minus the cost of revenue divided by revenue

hard costs—those fixed costs that result directly from the construction or sale of a particular unit; sometimes referred to as the direct construction costs or marketing "hards" and typically defined by a chart of accounts

hedging—process of protecting transactions or assets against future fluctuations in the market

historical cost—accounting principle that measures the value of an item by reference to its original purchase or acquisition price

horizontal expansion—growth achieved through the acquisition of other existing companies

income statement—financial statement that presents revenues, expenses, and resulting profit or loss, by conventional categories, for a particular period of time; also called an operating statement or a profit and loss statement

incremental costs—change in a cost or expense if one more unit is produced or sold

indenture—document that describes the features, terms, and conditions of a loan or bond

innovation—creation of something new and different; it is the specific instrument of entrepreneurship

insolvency—inability of a company to pay its debts and discharge its financial obligations

interest coverage ratio—measurement of liquidity that is equal to the earnings before interest and taxes or earnings before depreciation, earnings, and taxes, divided by required interest payments

interest rate—sum of money, generally expressed as an annual percentage of the principal, which is paid by a borrower to a lender. Such rates often depend on current market interest rates, the rate that an investor may expect to earn on his investment, on consumer/producers time preferences for current versus future consumption, the risk inherent in the loan, and the anticipated rate of inflation

investment banker—professional individual or company that can help companies optimize their capital structures, obtain financing, and seek acquisitions or divestitures

irrevocable letter of credit—absolute promise issued by a commercial bank, to pay a specific sum of money in the event that a certain condition or conditions are not met by a named third party

jumbo loans—permanent loans that exceed the current maximum loan amount established by federal regulations for governmental mortgage programs; loans that are greater than the conforming loan amount and limited in amount by the private investor

lead lender—lender that has accepted the responsibility for the administration and servicing of a participation loan, where two or more lenders have combined resources in order to make a loan

letter of credit—third-party obligation, based on credit, that builders sometimes use to secure performance or other obligation

leverage—financial term describing the multiplying effect from debt that owners get on the return on their investment; the use of debt capital to increase return on equity

limited liability company (LLC)—new form of incorporation that combines the advantage of flow-through taxation similar to a partnership or S corporation, with the limited liability protection enjoyed by all corporations; such organizations provide limited liability to investors, free transferability of ownership, continuity of life, and centralized management

line of credit—borrowing commitment or agreement with a commercial bank that makes a specific amount of money available to a borrower on a recurring or revolving basis

liquidity—ability of a company to pay current and short-term obligations

loan—a financial arrangement, with specific terms and conditions, evolving the exchange of money in return for the receiver's obligation to pay

loan-to-Value—ratio, typically expressed as a percentage, that measures the total loan amount divided by the appraised value of the property (loan amount ÷ current market value)

long-term planning—more general business planning that covers a three to five-year term; such planning is more loosely defined than short-term planning, which is generally restricted to three years

loss carry forward or back—ordinary corporate operating losses can be carried back, for tax purposes, to each of the preceding three years and forward for the next fifteen years to offset taxable income in those years. Losses carried back can often result in substantial income tax refunds where cyclical or shock losses follow periods of successful operation

management by exception—management concept that shifts the primary focus from what is happening at any given time to those exceptions from the established plans. Variance cost reporting is a primary tool for management by exception because it emphasizes those costs that are substantially over- or under-budget

management by objective (mbo)—management concept that uses goals and objectives, established by planning, to guide the actions of management in order to achieve a desired result in the future

management practice—practical application of management theory and principles within a particular industry or company

margin—measurement of profitability expressed as a percentage of profit to sales

market value statement—management statement similar to a balance sheet that lists fixed assets at their current net realizable market value sometimes used by management to evaluate the equity of a corporation following the liquidation of current assets; such statements have no basis in accounting and are merely used for evaluation

mortgage—note payable that uses real assets as collateral and requires periodic payments. Generally used to finance real estate, mortgages may be junior or senior in position; that is a first trust is senior to a second trust and would be satisfied first in the event of a default if it were secured by the same real property

merger—combining of two or more corporations in which case one survives and continues to provide the leadership and direction for the company

mezzanine debt—short-term (less than one year) and intermediate-term (one to five years) loans that are typically repaid after primary and secondary position lenders, but before unsecured lenders in the event of a liquidation

non-recourse loan—one that is not personally guaranteed by the borrowers

offering memorandum—document used, or sometimes required, to outline the terms of a solicitation for equity or a stock issue

operating expense—accounting term used to identify an expense that is not of the cost of goods sold; generally, an on-going expense necessary to operate a business

opportunity cost—estimated cost of an action relative to an alternative action that is made impossible by the given action

paid-in-capital—additional equity investment beyond the par value of a company's stock

participation loans—loans made by two or more lenders who have pooled their resources for the purpose of making a loan; such loans are often used by lenders to manage the perceived risks in a loan proposal, or to make a loan where the bank would otherwise be restricted by its loan limit to a single borrower

plan—detailed scheme or method of using resources to produce a desired result

pragmatic—based on facts rather than beliefs, ideas, or theories; conclusions based on an evaluation of cause and effect or needs and results

preferred stock—certificates of ownership with a right to fixed dividends, but no voting rights, that a corporation may issue to its equity investors

price/earnings ratio—ratio of common stock price to its earnings per share

prime rate—published interest rate at which banks will currently lend money to their most creditworthy customers

principal of consistency—accounting principle that dictates that a business should use the same accounting methods and procedures from one period to the next

private placement—sale of securities to a small number of sophisticated investors, as defined by the Securities and Exchange Commission

pro-active—that which supports activity or action

pro-forma income statement—standardized statement of projected revenue and expenses used by companies for the purposes of planning and presentation

projection—estimate of future performance made by planners, economists, and credit and securities analysts

public offering—sale of securities to the general public under the terms and conditions established by the Security and Exchange Commission

purchase money mortgage—"seller take-back financing" which is sometimes used in lieu of cash for a portion of the purchase price of a property; the seller finances a portion of the purchase price of a property and secures it with a mortgage which may or may not be subordinated to a construction loan including land advances and land development draws

qualified auditor's report—auditor's report that formally expressed concern for the continued survival of a company

quick ratio—ratio of the current assets (which include cash or assets that are quickly convertible to cash) divided by current liabilities

ratio analysis—standardized method of applying various formulas to business performance numbers, established by accounting records, in order to evaluate the liquidity, profitability, indebtedness, leverage, asset efficiency, or similar condition compared to previous performance or the performance of similar businesses in the same industry

real estate investment trust (REIT)—tax-exempt corporation that raises capital for real estate ventures by selling stock or commercial paper and passes at least 90 percent of its revenue directly to shareholders; in order to qualify, such corporations must include more than 100 stockholders with no fewer than six owning 50 percent or more of the trust, and 75 percent of their assets and income must be real estate related

retained earnings—amount of earnings retained by a business over a period of time that are equal to all of the past net income minus any dividends paid out

return on capital—measurement, expressed as a percentage, of the total investment earned by a business; net income divided by capital

return on equity—measurement, expressed as a percentage, of the owners' investment earned by a business; net income divided by equity

revolver—provision in a construction loan which allows the borrower to draw the loan down, pay it back, and thereby restore the loan limit for future borrowing; such provisions will typically reduce the fees paid by the borrower that are based on the total loan amount

revolving line of credit—continuing line of credit that does not have to be repaid at any given time; typically an unsecured loan used for general operating purposes

S corporation—unique corporate form that, among other things, provides for the direct pass-through of profits to its stockholders and limits the number of owners that can participate

secured loan—debt created to obtain money where interest is paid and collateral is pledged

short-term planning—more specific business planning that is typically restricted to a three-year term

silent partner—risk takers who are not interested in day-to-day operations; they are motivated by return and will take both debt and equity positions

soft costs—variable costs that result from business activity that are not directly attributable to the sales or construction process; indirect construction costs and marketing expenses are examples of soft costs

solvency—company's ability to pay long-term obligations generally based on positive equity; or the excess of the fair market value of total assets over total liabilities

solvency ratio—ratio measuring the relationship between debt and equity

sophisticated investor—one who has a substantial net worth, income, and can be presumed to understand business and financial statements

stakeholder—those who hold a stake or interest in a specific business or enterprise; those who may profit from or benefit from the success of a business or enterprise such as contractors, subcontractors, suppliers, brokers, and the like

starts—term used to describe the beginning of the direct construction process; most home builders use excavation or footings as the trigger for the start of the construction process

statement of changes in financial position—financial report that explains the changes in working capital or cash during a specific period of time; sometimes called the fund statement

strategic plan—program or carefully orchestrated scheme designed to achieve specific goals through the proper management of resources

strategy—plan of action resulting from careful thought that sets and guides actions designed to overcome an objective

tactical planning—that portion of the business planning process that deals with the implementation of strategies; operating policy, procedures, and processes all result from tactical planning

tax-free exchange—sale of a business or asset that is structured in a way that the seller incurs no immediate income tax liability

time value of money—concept that money today is more valuable than the same amount of money at some point in the future

transaction—external event involving the transfer of something of value between two or more entities

turnover—rate at which an asset such as inventory is used and replaced; it is expressed as the ratio of one year's revenue to the amount of the asset

underwriter—individual or company that, for a substantial fee, will guarantee the purchase of a full issue of stocks or bonds

unsecured loan—loan made without collateral based on the creditworthiness of the borrower; such loans are generally made based on a promise to repay and are established by a promissory note

variable costs—those costs that are not fixed and may change as a result of activity, efficiency, or volume

variable expense—any expense that changes with revenue

variance—in financial terms, it is the amount by which a financial parameter, such as cost, differs from its standard or budgeted value

variance purchase order—document used to record a deviation from the normal or standard purchasing requirements.

velocity—term used by home builders to indicate the pace of sales on a particular project; usually expressed as a number of sales per month

venture capital—funds that are reserved for, or invested in small or start-up companies

vertical analysis—relating the component parts of a financial statement to the total in the statements

vision—creative capacity or foresight to perceive the potential for an event or outcome based on current facts and conditions

window of opportunity—any limited time frame during which a favorable or promising combination of circumstances may produce advancement or improvement

working capital—current assets less current liabilities; considered a measurement of a company's ability to fund short-term operations

work in process inventory—that portion of inventory that consists of partially completed units and the associated labor, and material costs

REFERENCES

BOOKS

Accounting and Financial Management, 4th ed.
  Emma Shinn, BuilderBooks, Washington, D.C., 2002.
Accounting: A Basis for Business Decisions
  Meigs, McGraw Hill, Inc., New York, 1993.
Basic Business Management: A Guide for Small-Volume Home Builders
  Dorn Fowler, BuilderBooks, Washington D.C., 1998.
Benchmarking Your Business
  Jack Willenbrock, BuilderBooks, Washington, D.C., 2001.
The Business of Building: 2001 Cost of Doing Buisness Study
  2001 Cost of Doing Business Study
  National Association of Home Builders, Washington D.C., 2001.
Cash Flow Problem Solver
  Bryan E. Milling, Sourcebooks Trade, 1992.
Cash Rules
  Bill McGuinness, Kiplenger Books, Washington, D.C., 2000.
Common Sense Business in a Nonsense Economy
  Steven R. Galtry, Pfeiffer & Company, 1994.
The Ernst & Young Business Plan Guide
  Sigel, Ford & Bernsterin, John Wiley & Sons, Inc., New York, 1993.
The Essential Drucker
  Peter F. Drucker, Harper Business, New York, 2001.
Essentials of Business Budgeting
  Robert C. Finney, American Management Association, 1995.
Financial Essentials for Small Business Success
  Joseph Tabet and Jeffrey Slater, Upstart Publishing Co., Inc., Dover, New Hampshire, 1994.
Financial Management
  Eugene F. Brigham & Louis C. Gapenski, The Dryden Press, New York, 1991.
Financing for Small Builders and Developers
  National Association of Home Builders, BuilderBooks, Washington D.C., 1995.
Financial Statement Analysis
  Charles J. Waelfel, Probus Publishing Company, 1988.

Financing the Small Business
  Robert Sisson, Adams Media Corporation, Avon Massachusetts, 2002.
Going Public
  Martin Weiss, Liberty House, 1988.
How to Become Financially Successful by Owning Your Own Business
  Albert Lowry, Simon and Schuster, New York, 1981.
How To Raise Capital: Preparing and Presenting the Business Plan
  Grossman, Keller, Mitra, Raba & Robins, Dow Jones-Irwin, 1984.
How To Run A Small Business
  J. K. Lasser Institute, McGraw Hill, New York, 1993.
Innovation and Entrepreneurship
  Peter F. Drucker, Harper & Row Publications, New York, 1985.
Leveraged Finance: How To Raise and Invest Cash
  Mark Stevens, Prentice Hall, Inc., New Jersey, 1980.
Money Hunt
  Miles Spencer and Cliff Ennico, Harper Business, New York, 1999.
101 Business Ratios
  Sheldon Gates, McLean Publications, 1993.
The Probable MBA in Finance and Accounting
  John Leslie Livingstone, John Wiley & Sons, Inc., New York, 1992.
Short-Term America
  Michael T. Jacobs, Harvard Business School Press, 1991.
Strategic Financial Planning
  Harold Berman, Jr., The Free Press, 1980.
Strategic Planning for The Small Business
  Craig S. Rice, Bob Adams, Inc., 1990.
Strategic Planning That Makes Things Happen
  William C. Bean, Human Resource Development Press, 1993.
201 Great Ideas for Your Small Business
  Jane Appelgate, Bloomberg Press, Princeton, New Jersey, 1998.
Venture Capital Handbook
  David Gladstone, Prentice Hall, New Jersey, 1988.

ARTICLES

An Investigation of Management Practices Used In Small-Volume Home Building Companies of The United States
  Mark Hutchings, National Association of Home Builders, May 2002.
Cash-Flow Tips
  Thompson, *The Construction Industry Advisor,* Greenspon & Co., P.C., Fall 1997; 3.
Capital Ideas For Financing
  Sharon Nelton, *Nation's Business,* September 1996; P 18.
Controlling Overhead Costs
  Hugh H. Kerr, *The Contractor,* Summer 1996; P 1.

Form A Co-Op To Get Better Deals
Gerry Donohue, *Builder*, January 1996; P 299.
Pricing Opens The Door To Profit
Bill Lurz, *Professional Builder*, May 2002; P 36.
Secrets
Builder, August 1996; P 69.
Should You Be An LLC?
Frederick Y. Geber, *The Contractor*, Winter 1996; P 1.
Software Shows A Better Way To Analyze Land Acquisition
Jim Oakley, *Professional Builder*, October 1997; P 38.
Strategic Planning For Contractors: How to Plan for Success
Hugh H. Kerr, *The Contractor*, Fall 1996; P 3.
Sustaining A Competitive Advantage Poses Never-Ending Task For Builders
Edward Caldeira, *Professional Builder*, May 1997; P 36.
To Protect Your Assets, Think Ahead
Gary Kravitz, *RE Source*, Volume 207; P 2.
Will Your Next Lender Be On Wall Street?
Bill Hicks, *RE Source*, Volume 205a; P 2.

INDEX

A

Absorption rate, 27
Accelerated releases, 79
Accounting standards, 105
Accounts, chart of, 147–157
Accounts receivable, 100
Acquisition, development, and construction
   loan, *see also* Loan
   description of, 40, 46, 55
   elements of, 55
   loan-to-value ratio, 56–57, 69, 79
   participation loans, 59, 69
   revolver, 59–60, 69
Acquisitions, 46–47
Advertising
   cost considerations for, 78
   credits for, 75
   word-of-mouth, 78
Advisory boards, 90
Aggressive business plan, 31
Appraisal, 64, 69
Assets
   cross-collateralization, 66
   debt to asset ratio, 34
   efficiency of, 34
   equity to asset ratio, 34
   fixed, 100
   personal, *see* Personal assets protection
Assumptions, 26, 31
Attorneys, 83
Audit, 104–105, 140
Automobile insurance, 89

B

Balance sheet, 41
Bank(s)
   description of, 46
   investment, 49–51
   loans by, *see* Loan
Bank reconciliation, 109
Bankers, 108–109
Banking, 46
Bankruptcy, 115
Benchmark companies, 90, 102
Bidding, 77
Bonds, 45
Break-even analysis
   description of, 31–32
   ratio analysis, 32
Budget
   cash, 29–30, 102–103, 118, 139
   definition of, 102, 118
   description of, 28
   job-cost, 105
   purpose of, 102
   responsibility for preparing, 102
Builders, *see also* Company
   classification of, 33
   diversification by, 73
   partnerships among, 76–77
   sale of, 92
Business organization strategies, 25
Business plan
   achievable nature of, 31
   aggressive, 31
   attachments, 12–13
   benefits of, 5
   capitalization, 11, 13, 138–139
   case study, 121–142
   completed, 12–13
   conservative thinking in, 6
   copies of, 12
   cover sheet, 8
   description of, 3
   executive summary section of, 8, 13, 123
   financial plan, *see* Financial plan
   financial projections, 26, 139–140
   financial section of, 11–13, 139–140
   finished, 12–13
   format of, 7–8
   information sources, 6–7
   long-term planning in, 7, 13

Business plan (*Continued*)
  management structure, 10–11, 13, 134–137
  marketing plan, 8–9, 13
  operations section of, 9–10, 13, 130–134
  overview section of, 8, 13
  presentation of, 8–12
  professionals involved in creating, 6–7
  purpose of, 5–7
  realistic nature of, 31
  sample, 121–142
  short-term planning in, 7, 13
  statement of purpose, 8, 123–125
  table of contents of, 8
Buying cooperatives, 78

C
"C" corporation, 25
Capital
  debt, 40, 44–47
  equipment, 79–80
  equity, *see* Equity capital
  examination of, 25–26
  investment, 26, 79–80
  requirements, 39–40
  risk-based requirements, 57
  securing of, 40
  sources of, 39
  structure of, 25–26
  venture, 49–51
  working, 91, 99
Capitalization
  business plan description of, 11, 13
  sample, 125, 138–139
Capped guarantee, 96
Cash budget, 29–30, 102–103, 118, 139
Cash flow
  alterations of, 73
  cash budget use for increasing, 103
  conservation strategies for, 79–80
  construction loan draw schedule and, 59
  diversification of, 73–75
  factors that affect, 103, 118
  forecasting of, 30
  inadequate, 100
  maximizing of, 73–80
  statement of, 103
Cash management
  cash conservation, 79–80

cash flow, *see* Cash flow
cost overruns, 76–78
cost reduction, 76–78
description of, 73
Casual labor, 77
Certificate of insurance, 109
Change
  facilitation of, 15
  preparations for, 115, 118
Chart of accounts, 27, 147–157
Checks
  endorsement statements on, 110
  signers of, 109
  two-party, 110
Chief financial officer, 101
Closely held corporation, 53
Closing of loan, 66–67
Collateral marketing material, 78
Commercial banks
  description of, 46
  loans by, *see* Loan
Commercial finance companies, 48
Commitment for loan, 65–66, 69
Common stock, 41–42, 50, 53
Company, *see also* Builders
  capital structure of, 25–26
  classification of, 33
  culture of, 81–92, 126
  development for sale, 92
  failure of, 99–101
  insolvency of, *see* Insolvency
  liquidation of, 97
  operating efficiency of, 24–25
  productivity of, 24
  protection of, 114–115
  public offerings, 41–43
  reorganization of, 97
  sale of, 92
  stakeholders of, 17
  strategic planning by, *see* Strategic planning
Competition, 129
Competitive bidding, 77
Comptroller of the Currency, 48
Condominium associations, 91–92
Confidentiality agreement, 141–142
Conservative thinking, 6
Construction
  customer involvement in, 86, 134
  progress monitoring, 112–113

Construction financing
  loan, *see also* Acquisition, development, and construction loan; Loan
  overview of, 55–56
Construction/perm loan, 55–56, *see also* Loan
Consultants, 82–83, 130
Contingent liability, 65, 69, 96
Contracts, 85
Contribution margin, 32
Convertible debenture, 50, 53
Convertible preferred stock, 43
Cooperatives, 11, 78
Corporations, 25, 95
Cost(s)
  fixed, 31
  projection of, 28
  reduction of, 19, 24–25, 76–78, 131
  startup, 80
  variable, 31–32
Cost accounting, 103, 106–107, 118
Cost control system, 106
Cost overruns, 76–78
Cost-based pricing, 111, 118
Cover sheet, 8
Creative thinking, 18
Creditors, 111
Cross default, 66–67
Cross-collateralization, 66
Culture of company, 81–92, 126
Customer
  construction involvement by, 86, 134
  survey of, 114
Customer care, 20, 87–88, 128–129, 132
Cycle-time, 27, 74, 114

D
Debt capital, 40, 53
Debt financing
  description of, 44, 53
  intermediate-term, 45, 53
  long-term, 45–46, 53
  short-term, 45, 53
Debt ratio, 11, 26
Debt repayment, 100
Debt to asset ratio, 34
Debt to equity ratio, 34
Direct cost estimating, 105–106
Disclaimer, 26–27
Discounting, 101

Discounts, 75
Drucker, Peter F., 6, 15–16, 19
Duplicate payments, 110

E
Earth balance, 76
E-business strategies, 19, 132
Efficiency
  asset, 34
  operating, 24–25
Employees, *see also* Staff
  compensation for, 113
  insurance for, 88
  performance incentives for, 113
Endorsements, 95–96, 110
Engineers, 85, 134
Entrepreneur, 4, 50
Entrepreneurial strategies, 16
Equipment capital, 79–80
Equity
  assets to equity ratio, 34
  financing using, 41
  return on, 34
Equity capital
  description of, 41, 53
  insufficiency of, 99
  over-extending of, 91
  private investors, 43–44
  real estate investment trust, 49
  sale of stock, 41
  sources of, 44
Escrows, 74–75, 100
Estimating, 105–106
Executive summary, 8, 13, 123
External audit, 104

F
Feasibility analysis, 27–28, 83, 133
Federal Deposit Insurance Corporation, 48
Federal Reserve Board, 48
Final payments, 74–75, 100
Financial analyst, 35
Financial audit, *see* Audit
Financial consultant, 82–83
Financial controls
  accounting standards, 105
  audits, 104–105
  bank relationships, 108–109
  budget, *see* Budget
  description of, 101

Financial controls (*Continued*)
  direct cost estimating, 105–106
  financial manager's role in, 101
  financial statements, 104, 118
  income reserve accounts, 109
  job cost accounting, 106–107
  management reporting, 107
  miscellaneous, 109–111
  planning, 101–102
  purchase order, 106–108
  responsibility for, 101
Financial disclaimer, 26–27
Financial institutions, 48
Financial manager, 24, 35, 101, 108, 118
Financial plan
  accuracy of, 31
  break-even analysis, 31–34
  cash budget, 29–30
  chart of accounts, 27
  disclaimer in, 26–27
  facts presented in, 26–27
  life of project projections, 29
  pro-forma income statement, 29, 139
  purpose of, 28, 35
  realistic nature of, 31
  revenue strategies, 24
  risk assessments, 28
Financial planning
  description of, 23, 35
  documents, 29–31, 35
  feasibility analysis, 27–28
  importance of, 23, 101–102
  insolvency secondary to inadequacy of, 116
  process of, 27–29
  purpose of, 23, 35
  strategic, 24
Financial projections
  business plan presentation of, 26
  description of, 11–13
  sample, 139–140
Financial statements, 104, 118
Financing
  commercial finance companies, 48
  construction loan, *see* Loan
  debt, *see* Debt financing
  financial institutions, 48
  foreign investors, 52
  individual, 47–48
  investment banks, 49–51

letters of credit, 45, 68
life insurance companies, 48–49
line of credit, 45–46, 55, 61, 69
loan, *see* Loan
mortgage bankers, 51–52
pension funds, 49
proposal for, 143–146
public sources of, 47
real estate investment trust, 49
venture capital, 49–51
Fixed assets, 100
Fixed costs, 31
Floor checks, 86, 134
Focus groups, 114
Forecasting
  cash flow, 30
  management, 15
  sales, 27
Foreign investors, 52
Frame checks, 86, 134

G
GAAP, *see* Generally accepted accounting practices
Gap financing, 41, 43
General liability insurance, 88
Generally accepted accounting practices, 105, 118
Going public, 41–43, 47, 50, 97
Gross margin, 102, 111
Guarantees, 95–96

H
Homeowner, *see* Customer
Horizontal analysis, 104
Human resources strategies, 19, 131–132

I
Incentives
  options, 75
  performance, 113
Income
  reserves used to control, 109
  strategies for generating, 73–75
Income statement, pro-forma, 29, 139
Indebtedness, 34
Information sources, 6–7
Initial public stock offering, 50
Innovation
  benefits of, 15–16

definition of, 4
principles of, 4–5
sources of, 4–5
Insolvency
causes of, 116
definition of, 115
prevention of, 115–116
recovery from, 116–117
Insurance, 76, 88–89, 109
Interest reserves, 60, 69, 79
Intermediate-term debt financing, 45, 53
Internal audit, 104–105
Internet, 19
Inventory turnover, 74
Investment banks, 49–51
Investment capital, 26
Investors, 47–48
Irrevocable letter of credit, 68
Irrevocable trust, 96–97

J
Job cost accounting, 106–107, 118
Job cost budgets, 105
Joint ventures, 92–93

L
Land
acquisition strategies, 18, 130
development of, 18, 74, 83–84, 130
Earth balance, 76
location of, 83
revenue strategies for, 24
risk reduction, 83–84
Landscape watering, 78
Lead lender, 48
Leasing, 80
Lending
letters of credit, 45, 68
line of credit, 45–46, 55, 61, 69
loan, see Loan
process of, 62–67
Letters of credit, 45, 68
Leverage, 40, 44, 53, 91
Leverage ratio, 34, 44
Leveraged buy-out, 51
Liability
contingent, 65, 69, 96
product, 80
Liability insurance, 88
Lien releases, 109

Life insurance companies, 48–49
Life of project projections, 29
Limited liability company
characteristics of, 94
description of, 25, 41
personal asset protection using, 95
Limited partnership, 93–94
Line of credit, 45–46, 55, 61, 69
Liquidity, 33
Living trust, 96–97
Loan, see also Acquisition, development, and construction loan
agreement for, 66
application for, 63, 69
appraisal for, 64, 69
closing of, 66–67
commitment for, 65–66, 69
contingent liability for, 65, 69, 96
cross default provision for, 66–67
cross-collateralization requirement, 66
default of, 66–67
description of, 56
disbursement of, 57–59
draw schedule for, 57–59
initiation of, 62–63
interest reserves, 60
limitations, 56
loan-to-value ratio, 56–57, 69, 79
negotiating of, 55
participation, 59, 69
progress payments, 79
prospecting of, 62
revolver, 59–60, 69
risk-based capital requirements, 57
set asides, 60
source of, 62
underwriting of, 63–65, 69
Loan committee, 65
Loan officers, 108
Loan proposal, 61–62, 143–146
Loan with warrants, 50–51, 53
Loan-to-value ratio, 56–57, 69, 79
Long-term debt financing, 45–46, 53
Long-term planning, 7–8, 13
Lumber lists, 76

M
Management
business plan description of, 10–11
compensation strategies for, 10–11

Management (*Continued*)
  financial reporting, 107
  forecasting by, 15
  product development strategies, 18
  strategic planning and thinking by,
    19–20, 132
  structure of, 10, 13, 134–138
Management consultant, 82
Market strategies
  description of, 18
  revenue increases, 24
  sample, 130–131
Marketing consultant, 82
Marketing plan, 8–9, 13, 129
Market-value statement, 103
Mechanic liens, 109–110
Mergers, 46–47
Model home rebates, 75
Mortgage bankers, 51–52
Mortgage loans, 46

N
National Association of Home Builders
  chart of accounts, 147–157
Non-standard options, 74
Notes, 100

O
Office of Thrift Supervision, 48
On-site construction managers
  floor checks by, 86, 134
  frame checks by, 86, 134
  oversight inspections by, 87, 134
  well-qualified, 85
On-site sales manager, 88, 112
Operating efficiency, 24–25
Operations section of business plan, 9–10,
    13, 130–134
Options
  incentives for, 75
  pricing of, 111
  strategies for, 74
Over expansion, 100
Over-leverage, 91
Over-pricing, 111, 118
Oversight inspections, 87, 134

P
Partial guarantee, 96
Participation loans, 59, 69

Partnerships
  meetings of, 114
  programs for, 76–77
Payroll tax, 90
Pension funds, 49
Performance incentives, 113
Personal assets protection
  corporation, 95
  endorsements and guarantees limited or
    denied, 95–96
  irrevocable trust, 96–97
  limited liability company, 95
  liquidating, selling, or reorganizing of
    company, 97
  living trust, 96–97
  overview of, 94–95
Personal holding companies, 97
Plan, *see* Business plan; Financial plan
Planning
  employee involvement in, 113
  financial, *see* Financial planning
  foundation of, 3
  importance of, 3, 82
  long-term, 7–8
  purpose of, 3
  short-term, 7–8
  strategic, *see* Strategic planning
Post-settlement service, 88
Preferred stock, 42–43, 50, 53
Pricing
  cash flow and, 73–74
  control of, 74
  cost-based, 111, 118
  improper, 99
  over-pricing, 111, 118
  setting of, 111
  strategies for, 19, 131
  under-pricing, 111, 118
Private investors, 43–44
Product development strategies
  collateral marketing material, 78
  description of, 18
  revenue increases, 24
  sample, 127, 131
Productivity, 24, 75
Profitability
  company involvement, 113–114
  construction progress monitoring,
    112–113
  description of, 33–34

focus groups, 114
performance incentives, 113
sales, 111–112
strategies for maintaining, 111–115
surveys, 114
Pro-forma income statement, 29, 139
Progress payments, 79
Projections
costs, 28
description of, 26
financial, 11–13, 26
life of project, 29
Property damage insurance, 88
Public offerings, 41–43, 47, 50, 97
Public relations strategies, 20, 132
Purchase order, 106–108
Purchase-money mortgage
accelerated releases, 79
definition of, 67, 69
subordinated, 67–69

Q
Quality building program, 84–87, 133–134

R
Ratio analysis, 32, 35, 110
Real estate investment trust, 49
Recycling, 77
REIT, *see* Real estate investment trust
Reserve accounts, 109
Retaining walls, 84
Return on assets, 34
Return on equity, 34
Return on investment, 40
Revenue, 24
Revolver, 59–60, 69
Risk
assessment of, 28
leverage and, 44
management of, 80–81
staffing considerations, 80–81
Risk reduction methods
advisory boards, 90
benchmark companies used as guide, 90
company culture, 81–82
condominium associations, 91–92
consultants, 82–83, 130
customer involvement, 86
description of, 80–81
engineers, 85

feasibility study, 83, 133
floor checks, 86, 134
frame checks, 86, 134
insurance, 88–89
land development, 83–84
leveraging, 91
oversight inspections, 87, 134
payment policy, 90–91
planning, 82
quality assurance program, 86
quality building program, 84–87,
133–134
safety, 87
tax obligations, 89–90
working capital adequacies, 91
workplace safety, 87

S
"S" corporation, 25
Safety, 87
Sale(s)
evaluation of, 112
forecasts for, 27
promotion of, 111–112
steps involved in, 112
Sale of stock, 41
Sales manager, 88, 112
Sales tax, 106
Scope of work, 85
Securities and Exchange Commission, 42,
47
"Seller take-back financing," *see* Purchase-
money mortgage
Set asides, 60
Short-term debt financing, 45, 53
Short-term planning, 7–8, 13
Soil
engineers for, 85
poor quality, 78
Sole proprietorship, 25
Solid waste disposal, 77
Staff, 80–81, 85, *see also* Employees
Stakeholders, 17
Standard options, 74, 111
Startup costs, 80
Statement of cash flows, 103
Statement of purpose, 8, 123–125
Status reporting, 107
Stock
common, 41–42, 50, 53

Stock (*Continued*)
    preferred, 42–43, 50, 53
    rights of, 43
    sale of, 41
Strategic planning
    benefits of, 15
    change identified by, 15
    cost reduction, 19, 131
    creative thinking stimulated by, 18
    customer care, 20
    definition of, 15, 22
    e-business, 19, 132
    financial, 24
    human resources, 19, 131–132
    land acquisition and development, 18,
        130
    management, 19, 132
    market, 18, 130–131
    needs determination, 17–20
    ongoing need for, 21–22
    pricing, 19
    process of, 16–17, 22
    product development, 18, 131
    public relations, 20, 132
    sample, 130–132
    steps involved in, 16–17, 22
Strategic thinking, 20–21
Structural engineer, 85
Subordinated purchase-money mortgage,
    67–69
Surveys, 114

T
Tax deductible, 40
Taxes, 89–90
Terminology, 159–168
Thrifts, 48, 56, 69
Title insurance, 89
Trust
    irrevocable, 96–97
    living, 96–97
    real estate investment, 49
Two-party checks, 110

U
Umbrella insurance, 89
Under-pricing, 111, 118
Underwriting of loan, 63–65, 69
Uniform contracts, 85

V
Variable costs, 31–32
Variance purchase order, 108
Venture capital, 49–51
Vertical analysis, 104
Vision, 15

W
Waste reduction, 25, 77
Watering of landscape, 78
Working capital, 91, 99
Work-package takeoff, 105
Workplace safety, 87